The
MARRIAGE LICENSE BONDS
of
WESTMORELAND COUNTY, VIRGINIA
From 1786 to 1850

Listed and Indexed
by
Stratton Nottingham

CLEARFIELD COMPANY

Originally Published
[Onancock, Virginia, 1928]

Reprinted
Genealogical Publishing Co., Inc.
Baltimore, 1975

Reprinted for
Clearfield Company, Inc., by
Genealogical Publishing Co., Inc.
Baltimore, Maryland
1992, 1995

Library of Congress Cataloging in Publication Data
Nottingham, Stratton.
  The marriage license bonds of Westmoreland County, Virginia,
1786-1850, listed and indexed.
  Reprint of the 1928 ed. published in Onancock, Va.
  1. Marriage licenses—Westmoreland Co., Va.
2. Westmoreland Co., Va.—Genealogy.   I. Title.
F232.W4N9   1975   929'.3755'24   74-18047
ISBN 0-8063-0651-3

Made in the United States of America

THE MARRIAGE LICENSE BONDS
of
WESTMORELAND COUNTY, VIRGINIA
From 1786 to 1850

Westmoreland County, formed in 1653 from Northumberland County, is one of the early water-front counties of Virginia forming the Northern Neck group. The records of Westmoreland contain much of the history of the great families of Virginia, Washington, Lee, Monroe, &c., and these and many other names of equal interest frequently appear in this list. In a good many instances where the marriage bond has been lost, proof of marriage is shown by the "consent" of either the contracting parties or their parents, in some cases giving the date of birth, place of marriage, &c. These have also been included in this list.

The marriage bonds here listed are on file in the Clerk's Office of Westmoreland County.

The compiler wishes to acknowledge his sincere appreciation to Mr. Albert Stuart, Clerk of the Court, for his valuable assistance and unfailing courtesy.

Abbott, James & Fanny Jeffries 23 Dee. 1809, John S. Tapscott sec.

Adams, Alexander & Virginia C. Lowe, dau. Mary Lowe 27 Aug. 1838
  James B. Murphy sec.
Adams, John & Winnaen Baley 11 Jan. 1841, Caphius Newman sec.

Adkins, Valentine & Alphebe Lucas 2 Jan. 1837, Zachariah W.
  Franklin sec.

Alderson, James & Jane Baber 23 June 1814, Wesley Porter sec.

Allen, John & Fanny Mealey, dau. Daniel Mealey --- 1823, Robert
  Bailey sec.

Alton, John & Lucinda Butler, dau. Mary Butler 6 Feb. 1804
  Vincent Berrick sec.

Alverson, Frederick & Caty Doulman 23 Apr. 1800, John Hill sec.
Alverson, Frederick & Nancy Carroll 5 Mar. 1810, John Gregory sec.
Alverson, Frederick & Margaret Short 14 Sept 1833, William Branson
  sec.
Alverson, Frederick & Mary F. Kirk 26 Mar 1849, John C. Gregory sec.
Alverson, John & Sally Hall 19 Dec 1826, Clarke Short sec.
Alverson, John & Martha McGuire 7 Feb 1833 - John Hazard sec.
Alverson, Teliff, of Richmond County & Alice Brinham 11 Nov 1789
  William Coward sec.
Alverson, Zachariah & Keziah Burgess, wid. 22 -- 1791, Nathaniel
  Collingsworth sec.

Ambrus, Elijah & Catherine Ollive 18 Mar. 1818, William Allen sec.

Ambers, Elijah & Sally Olliv 30 Jan. 1827, James Morris sec.

Ambrose, Elijah & Sally Wilson 1 Aug 1831, William Wilson sec.

Anderson, James F. & Juliet A. Wallace 19 Apr 1838, Thomas Sandy
  sec.
Anderson, John F. & Ann M. Sanford 15 Mar 1837, William A.
  Harrison sec
Anderson, Robert & Treasy Carrell 25 Apr. 1805, James King sec.
Anderson, William & Ann King 21 Dec.1766, William Middleton sec.
Anderson, William & Peggy Fisher 4 Feb. 1811, Thomas King sec.
Anderson, William & Lucy Jeffries 4 Apr. 1826, Henry Lumpkin sec.
Anderson, William & Jane Sanford 26 Nov. 1632, Richard H. Sanford
  sec.

Annidal, Andrew & Delitha Johnson, dau. Thomas Johnson, 27 Jan.
  1827, William Jett sec.
Annadale, Robert & Mary Good 31 May 1798, James Thomas sec.
Annandale, Samuel C. & Cynthia Branson 8 Oct. 1811, John Collins
  Worth sec.
Annadale, Thomas & Penny Mothershead 23 Jan. 1790, David Annadale
  sec.
Anadale, Thomas & Ann C. Poor, dau. Thomas Poor, 10 Jan. 1824,
  Alexander Weaver sec.

Annandale, William & Elizabeth Dodd 18 June 1805, Spencer Feagett sec.

Annodale, David & Winifred Clayton 29 Mar 1788, Thomas Annodale sec.
Annodale, David & Mary Poor, dau. Charles Poor, 26 Aug. 1794, Joseph Annodale sec.
Annodale, Joseph & Geane Carter 12 Aug. 1799, David Annodale sec.

Anton, Benj: & Desty M. Howson 11 Jan. 1845, Thomas Howell sec.
Anton, Fleet & Frances Spurling 7 June 1830, William Spurling sec.
Anton, Robert & Elizabeth Howson 25 July 1816, James Gregory sec.
Anton, Robert & Elizabeth Douglas 11 Dec 1844, Samuel Anton sec.
Anton, Samuel & Susannah Gregory 20 July 1824, Thomas Howell sec.
Anton, Samuel & Elizabeth Gregory 24 Apr 1832, Thomas Howell sec.

Antoney, James & Fanney Weaver 6 Sept 1816, Campbell Teet sec.

Anthony, James C. & Mary Lee 14 July 1808, Baldwin M. Lee sec.
Anthony, James & Rebecca Billins 5 July 1809, Youel F.Howsen sec.
Anthony, James & Elizabeth Goode 31 Dec 1811, William Tate sec.
Anthony, James & Elizabeth Senders 4 Oct. 1825, James Brown sec.
Anthony, John & Kettuar Thomas 2 Oct. 1821, Samuel Davis sec.
Anthony, Robert & Lettice Gregory 1 Dec 1788, Thomas Gregory sec.
Anthony, William & Susannah McKenney 26 Oct. 1819, Marcus C. Harvey sec.

Arnest, John, of Baltimore, & Anne Martin Maund, dau. H. L. Maund, 16 Jan. 1810, John W. Jones sec.
Arnest, Thomas M. & Emily M. Beale 5 Nov. 1839, Richard L. T. Beale sec.

Arnold, Weedon & Mary Morriss, dau. Charles Morriss 25 Dec 1787 Caleb Smith sec.
Arnold, William & Mary E. Deatley 8 Apr. 1823, James E.Deatley sec.

Asbury, Henry & Sally Moxley, wid. 9 Apr 1796, William Bragg sec.
Asbury, John & Patty Self, dau. Stephen Self, 20 June 1792, William Self sec.
Asbury, Richard & Nancy B. Yeatman, dau. Nancy H. Yeatman, 19 Nov. 1848, William P. Crabb sec.
Asbury, William & Mary Muse, dau. Thomas Muse, 14 Apr. 1806, Richard Efford sec.

Askins, Benjamin & Jane Grant 15 Nov. 1803, Jeremiah Jeffries sec.
Askins, Charles S. & Nancy Olive 17 Apr. 1820, Stephen Olive sec.
Askins, William & Sally Beale, dau. Samuel Beale, 16 Dec. 1812 Willis Garner sec.

Asting, Moses & Polly Lauder 20 Apr 1826, Thomas Sanders sec.

Aston, Blain & Priscy Jelson 24 Jan 1814, Edmund Tate sec.
Aston, Jeremiah & Elizabeth Lewis 6 Mar 1837, Jacob Aston sec.

Ashton, Allen & Elizabeth Lucas 24 Dec. 1793, Leonard Lucas sec.

Ashton, Alexander & Louisa Micon, dau. John H. Micon. 13 Jan 1835
    Robert Brandicon & Thomas L. Muse sec.
Ashton, Basil & Hannah Lucas 29 May 1833, Joseph S. Lyell sec.
Ashton, Blane & Susan Sorrel 14 Jan 1823, Lawrence Ashton sec.
Ashton, Burditt & Jane Thompson -- Feb. 1829, Rodham Ashton sec.
Ashton, David & Nancy Bowden 30 Dec 1790, Bennett McGuy sec.
Ashton, David & Betty Newgent, wid. 22 June 1796, John Pilsbury sec.
Ashton, George & Elizabeth Jett, dau. William H. Jett, 26 May 1809
    William H. Jett, Jr. sec.
Ashton, George & Julia Tate 3 Jan 1844, Blain Ashton sec.
Ashton, George D. & Catherine Roberta Rose Hodge 23 Jan 1823, S.H.
    Brown sec.
Ashton, Kelsick & Mary Tate 10 Dec 1845, Ludwell Ashton sec.
Ashton, Henry & Lucy Weeks 7 July 1829, Blain Ashton sec.
Ashton, John & Betsey Ashton 20 Jan 1836, Lawrence Ashton sec.
Ashton, John & Zenoba Ashton 28 Jan. 1843, Blain Ashton sec.
Ashton, Richard & Jenny Lawrence 23 Dec 1797, Lawrence Ashton sec.
Ashton, Rodham & Polly Sanford -- Jan. 1818, Lawrence Ashton sec.
Ashton, Rodham & Lucinda Davis, dau. Sally Davis, 6 Feb. 1838,
    Henry Clarke sec.
Ashton, Tasker & Eliza Corbin 18 Jan 1848, Abraham Hall sec.

Atkins, Ritchie & Jane Strother 5 Feb 1816, Christopher Deatley sec.

Attwell, Francis & Fanny McCave 5 Apr 1796, John Bulger sec.
Attwell, Thomas & Molley Spence Griggs, dau. Mary Griggs, 17 Nov.
    1792, Henry Griggs sec.
Atwill, John L. & Mary Norwood, dau. John Norwood, 30 Sept. 1833
    Charles H. Sanford sec.
Atwill, James K. & Eliza J. Muse 11 Feb. 1836, Joseph S. Lyell sec.
Atwill, Samuel B. & Jane A. Brown 20 Dec 1842, Thomas Brown sec.

Ayres, James & Elizabeth Doleman 26 Dec. 1821, Henry H. Hazard sec.

Baber, Claiburne & Hannah C. Crabb (not dated - In bundle marked
    "1803") William P. Crabb sec. (Bond signed but not filled
    in)
Baber, Dabney & Jane Crabb 14 Dec. 1809, Benedict Crabb sec.

Bailey, James H. & Harriott McNeil 16 Sept 1807, John Goode sec.
Bailey, John & Nancy Mathany 11 Sept. 1810, Jeremiah Jeffries sec.
Bailey, John L. & Elizabeth R. Cox, dau. James Cox, 13 Dec 1828,
    Richard J. Thompson sec.
Bailey, John H. & Temperance Beale 25 Mar 1834, Sydnor Beale sec.
Bailey, Reuben & Mary Sutton 8 Dec. 1795, John S. Sutton sec.
Bailey, Robert S. & Roberta Ann Cox 12 Nov. 1844, William H.
    Benson sec.

Baker, Richard & Sarah Row 11 Jan 1788, William Roe sec.

Ball, Edmund & Judy Newman, dau. Samuel Newman, 24 Apr. 1844,
    James Newman sec.
Ball, John & Anna Thomas 8 Dec. 1789, William Airs sec.
Ball, Spencer & Betsey Landon Carter, dau. Robert Carter of Nomony
    Hall, born 25 Oct. 1765 - 26 Mar. 1788, Henry Lee sec.
Ball, Spencer & Elizabeth Thomas, dau. James Thomas 11 Jan. 1793

John Ball sec.

Balmain, Andrew & Nancy C. Ray, wid. 25 Mar. 1794, Henry Washington
    sec.

Balthmore, Thomas & Hannah Self 12 Dec. 1837, Edward Smith sec.

Baldison, Berryman & Elizabeth Jones 25 Dec. 1809, John Balderson
    sec.
Balderson, David & Susan Mothershead 27 Dec. 1849, William L.
    Mothershead sec.
Balderson, Ebenezer & Anne Clark 19 Dec. 1791, John Nash sec.
Balderson, James B. & Feisin F. Franklin 17 Oct. 1826, John
    Morris sec.
Balderson, James P. & Elizabeth Hardwick 27 Dec 1841, Henry Curtis
    sec.
Balderson, John & Caty Edmonds -- 1807, Vincent Edmonds sec.

Bane, Thomas & Elizabeth Redeck 9 Oct. 1793, William Spurling sec.

Barnett, Henry & Alleymenty Carroll 31 Jan. 1791, Richard Barnett
    sec.
Barnett, John & Hannah Curtis, dau. Rebecka Curtis 17 Nov. (87¶
    Richard Sanford sec. Badly damaged.
Barnett, Joseph & Louisa Holliday, dau. Feilding Holliday, 28 Nov.
    1831, John B. Carroll sec.
Barnett, Levi & Martha Pope, dau. John B. Pope, 7 Oct. 1839,
    Richard Pritchett sec.
Barnett, William & Jane Smith 2 Jan. 1811, William B. Smith sec.

Barns, Charles & Hannah Neale 5 Nov. 1806, LeRoy Dobyns sec.

Barrett, John & Elizabeth Briscoe 10 Mar. 1812, Mason B. Dodd sec.
Barrett, William & Elizabeth Cole, - Consent of Elizabeth & Peggy
    Cole dated 27 May 1822, Witt: by Samuel J. Booth - Bond
    signed but not filled in - Samuel J. Booth sec.

Barrick, John & Mary Beann, wid. 12 July 1793, Moses Self sec.

Barrot, John & Elizabeth Mullins -- Nov. 1801 (bond signed but
    not filled in) John Mullins sec.
Barrot, John & Mary Parress 21 Feb. 1833, Nicholas Quisenbury sec.
Barrott, William & Felicia Pegg 31 Dec. 1814 ----

Barrok, George G. & Maria James 11 Feb. 1820, Thomas James sec.
Barrock, Vincent & Elizabeth Weeks 11 Dec 1800, Robert Hall sec.

Barber, Cornelius W. of the City of Baltimore, & Elizabeth Plummer
    12 May 1845, James Nelson sec.
Barber, Thomas & Lucy Mothershead, dau. Isabella Mothershead, 6
    Nov. 1811, James Yeatman sec.

Bartlett, Henry & Carlisle E. Reamy 11 Nov. 1828, Thomas Miller sec.
Bartlett, James & Sarah Troop 27 Jan 1808, William Boying sec.

Bartlett, Joel & Sally Wilson 24 Dec 1821, Lemuel G. Sandy sec.
Bartlett, Thomas & Polly Mothershead dau. John Mothershead, 4 Jan.
   1815, William Mothershead sec.

Barkly, James & Hannah Brinnon 14 Dec. 1810, John Redman sec.

Barker, Daniel & Lucy Smith dau. Ann Smith, 20 Oct. 1803, William
Barker, John&cMargaret Quisenbury 22 June 1738, Daniel Barker sec.
Barker, John & ------ Gutridge 26 Mar. 1810, John Peede sec.
Barker, John & Frances Deatley 23 Mar. 1835, Richard E. Deatley sec.
Barker, Joseph & Elizabeth Hall 4 Dec. 1610, William Hall sec.
Barker, Sandy A. & Amelia Ann Moor, dau. Mary Moor, 12 Jan. 1837,
   Tounsend Barker sec.
Barker, Townsend & Alcy Crask 16 Nov. 1842, William Hull sec.
Barker, William & Mary Marks 16 Sept. 1828, Campbell Teet sec.
Barker, William & Mary V. Carpenter 14 Apr. 1849, Frederick Poor sec.

Bashaw, Warner & Aggatha Wright, wid. 2 May 1791

Basham, Epephroditus & Ann Robinson 26 Feb. 1798, John Sanford sec.

Bassett, Burwell & Elizabeth McCarty, dau. Daniel McCarty, 10 Jan.
   1788, Daniel McCarty, Jr. sec.

Bassye, Thomas Pope & Hannah Lee Turberville, dau. Martha Turberville
   15 May 1804, Thomas Legg sec.

Batten, Richard & Eliza Edwards 26 Sept. 1808, Thomas Gregory sec.
Batton, Robert & Priscilla Muir 6 Dec 1825, Vincent J. Branson sec.
Batten, William & Minty Alverson 7 Oct. 1835, William T. Branson sec.

Baxter, Bennett & Ann Robinson Jones, dau. Thomas Jones, 22 Apr.
   1794, Thomas Muse sec.
Baxter, Joseph & Ann Maria Deatley, dau. Matthew Deatley, 29 July
   1744, William Hutt sec.

Bayne, John & Ellen Tiffey 28 Nov. 1814, Richard Bayne sec.
Bayne, Matthew & Caty Harrison, wid. 3 Aug. 1789, Jacob Vigor sec.
Bayne, Richard V. & Elizabeth Marmaduke, dau. Vincent Marmaduke
   7 Dec. 1846, M. M. Marmaduke sec.

Beazley, Cornelius & Jane R. Rust 3 Nov. 1807, William Rice sec.

Beale, Henry & Darcus Garner 14 June 1799, Solomon Redman sec.
Beale, James & Ann Elmore 19 Apr. 1826, Smith Beale sec.
Beale, John C. & Sally B. Butler, 22 May 1820, Robert Long sec.
Beale, John C. & Elizabeth Chew 19 May 1825, S. S. Hall sec.
Beale, John & Fanny Minor 19 Dec. 1826, Smith Beale sec.
Beale, Reuben, bro. of William C. Beale, & Eliza Taylor Turberville
   28 Apr. 1800, Orrick Chilton sec.
Beale, Samuel, Jr. & Susannah Smith 29 Dec. 1791
Beale, Samuel, Jr. & Judah Middleton 9 June 1798, Henry Beale sec.
Beale, Samuel & Alice Harris 9 Oct. 1792, Daniel Boyer sec.

Beale, Samuel & Nancy Garner, dau. James Garner, 27 Jan. 1795, Job
    Self sec.
Beale, Smith & Ann Beale 13 May 1837, Thomas C. Beacham sec.
Beale, Smith & Catherine J. Elmore 19 Dec 1826, John H. Elmore sec.
Beale, Stephen L. & Harriet Elmore 20 Mar. 1832, William Carey sec.
Beale, Sydnor & Sarah A. M. Parks, dau. Arthur Parks, 22 Jan. 1838
    Henry Beale, Jr. sec.
Beale, Thomas T. & Eliza S. Wheeler 17 Jan. 1846, Benjamin Short sec.
Beale, William S. & Frances G. Garner 29 Dec. 1823, Willis Garner sec

Beane, John & Ann King, wid. 22 Mar. 1788, William Harrison sec.

Beacham, James W. & Bridget Parks, dau. Arthur Parks, 29 Nov. 1828
    George L. Beacham sec.
Beacham, Nathaniel & Martha Spurling 30 Dec. 1830, John Hazard sec.
Beacham, Robert J. & Jane Ann English, dau. John English, 2 Jan.
    1850, George Courtney sec.
Beacham, Thomas & Betsy Elmore, dau. John Elmore 16 Jan. 1823, John
    B. Murphy sec.

Beckwith, Barnes & Elizabeth P. Martin 23 Jan. 1805, Robert L.
    Hipkins sec.

Beddoo, John & Nancey Balderson 20 Sept. 1800, Jacob Miller sec.
Beddoe, John & Julily Jones 3 Jan. 1838, James Jones sec.
Beddo, Nathaniel & Christine Cook, dau. Elizabeth Massey, -- May
    1842, John Massey sec.
Beddoo, Newton & Susan Henage 1 Nov. 1848, James A. Weaver sec.
Beddo, William & Fanny Hennage 11 Apr. 1798, Benj: Beamham sec.

Bell, Charles & Winifrid C. Rust 15 Jan. 1794, Leroy Hillard
Bell, Charles, Jr. & Hannah Rust 15 Jan. 1794, Leroy Hillard sec.
Bell, Charles L. & Jane M. Wright 3 May 1827, William Wright sec.

Bellfield, Thomas M. & Frances F. Sandford, dau. Sebbella Sandford
    21 Nov. 1821, David C. Belfield sec.
Belfield, Thomas M.,Jr. & Eliza J. McClannahan 22 Nov. 1841, Edwin
    Hutt sec.

Benson, William H. & Martha F. Redman 30 Mar. 1833, Edward Cox sec.

Bennett, Jesse & Jemima Cole 30 Oct. 1787, Ebenezer Morse sec.
Bennett, Richard & Alice Middleton 23 Dec. 1788, George Middleton
    sec.
Bennett, Robert & Jane Lefevre 26 July 1800, Elisha Spurling sec.

Berryman, Alexander & Catherine Berryman 22 Apr. 1812, Newton
    Berryman sec.
Berryman, Gerard B. & Alice Quisenbury 21 Oct. 1790, Thomas N.
    Berryman sec.
Berryman, James & Margaret Sthreshly 15 Oct. 1787, Thomas
    Sthreshley sec.
Berryman, Samuel & Ann Berkley 28 Feb. 1792, Edward Sanford sec.
Berryman, William & Nancy Beal Self 13 June 1804, Dozier Lyell sec.

Bevelton, Francis & Mary Lewis Sanders 26 May 1798, Philip Peede
  sec.
Bevelton, Francis & Ellen Yardley 18 Dec 1834, Walker Winkfield sec.
Bevelton, George & Penny Lucas 31 Dec. 1811, Stephen S. Mothershead
  sec.

Billins, John & Elizabeth Reynolds 13 Nov. 1789, Thomas Gregory sec.

Blackwell, John & Frances Parker 28 Nov. 1814, Alexander Parker sec.

Bland, James & Ursula Gordon, wid. 12 Feb. 1788, James McNeil sec.
Bland, James & Alice Barnett 12 May 1797, Joseph Hague sec.
Bland, James & Sarah Coleman 18 July 1817, Sam. Coleman sec.

Blancett, Rodham & Jane Brown 10 Apr. 1789, William Brown sec.

Blundell, Jeremiah & Ann Pomroy 15 Jan. 1795, Thomas Blundell sec.

Booth, James & Susanna Crenshaw 24 July 1797, David Crenshaw sec.
Boothe, Samuel J. & Mary W. Wright 27 June 1817, William Brann sec.

Boon, George & Mary Burkley 29 Nov. 1805, Thomas Muse, Jr.

Bowcock, Henry & Catherine Monroe 28 July 1819, Richard Monroe sec.
Bowcock, Henry P. & Maria Smith 21 Jan. 1822, John F. Smith sec.
Bowcock, Henry P. & Ann M. Cox, dau. James L. Cox, 21 Nov. 1837,
  W. G. Walker sec.

Bowie, John C. & Sarah A. Cox, dau. James L. Cox, 11 July, 1836,
  George C. Harvey sec.

Bowen, John & Rachel Drake, dau. Rose Drake, 5 Feb. 1787, John
  Drake sec.
Bowen, John & Maria Marshall 20 Dec..1837, Thomas Parker sec.
Bowen, John & Ruth Mozingo 25 Dec. 1844, Thomas Mozingo sec.
Bowen, Jonathan & Sarah Paris 29 Dec. 1811, George Newman sec.
Bowen, Kelly H. & Mariah Fegget 17 Dec. 1827, John Pullin sec.
Bowen, Thomas & Ann Burr 8 Feb. 1837, Richard Dozier sec.

Bowing, James L. & Susan Wilson 3 Jan. 1837, John L. Carter sec.
Bowing, Jesse & Nancy Kelly, dau. Molly Kelly, 24 Mar. 1810
  George Wapel sec.
Bowing, Thomas & Molly Hinson (not dated - in bundle marked "1803")
  Jonah Hinson & William Bowing sec.

Bragg, Henry H. & Mary Ann Askins dau. Nancy G. Askins, 18 Jan.
  1848, J. B. Thrift sec.
Bragg, Ishmael & Mary Dozier 7 Jan. 1823, Thomas M. Bragg sec.
Bragg, John & Caty Garner 9 Dec. 1824, George Jeffries sec.

Brawner, Henry & Ann Caddeen 21 Dec. 1811, John Omohundro sec.
Brawner, James & Kitty Anthoney 8 Jan. 1838, John Beddoo sec.
Brawner, Capt. John & Jane Clark 13 Jan. 1827, George Watson sec.

Brawner, William & Fanney Nash 10 Jan. 1920, Spencer Mullins sec.

Bramham, Vincent & Hannah Bushrod Smith 28 Dec 1793, Baldwin B.
    Smith sec.

Brann, James & Susanna Garner 9 Jan. 1817, Joseph Elmore sec.
Brann, Reuben & Frances Garlick 11 Feb. 1797, William Garlick sec.
Brann, Richard & Jane Curk (Kirk?) 16 Nov. 1805, Jeremiah Jeffries
    sec.
Brann, Samuel & Polley Thomas 15 Jan. 1810, Reubin Reynolds sec.
Brann, Stephen & Peggy Hawkins 15 Oct. 1807, Jeremiah Davis sec.
Brann, William, Jr.&Keziah Jewell dau. Eliza Jewel, 19 Sept. 1801
    Reubin Spurling sec.
Brann, William, Jr. & Augilla Morris 31 Jan. 1828, William Gilbert
    sec.
Brann, William & Jane Elmore 9 Feb. 1833, David B. Taylor sec.
Brann, William & Frances Y. McKenney 26 Feb. 1839, Joseph McKenney
    sec.

Branson, John M. & Ann R. Rice 17 Mar. 1828, Newyear C. Branson sec.
Branson, Newyear & Fanny Brinnon 11 Oct. 1810 Thomas Barber sec.

Brandican, J. Robert, of King George County, & Ann M. Anderson
    29 July 1846, Alexander Ashton sec.

Brewer, James & Betsey Turnbull 10 Dec. 1790, John Brewer sec.
Brewer, James, Jr. & Betsy Spence 3 Dec. 1792, John Brewer sec.
Brewer, James & Nancy Richardson 18 Oct. 1802, William Dishman sec.
Brewer, Robert & Sarah Peed 6 Feb. 1816, John Peed sec.
Brewer, Samuel & Alice Sanders 6 Dec. 1796, John Brewer sec.
Brewer, Thomas & Mary Hinson 4 Jan. 1821, Austin Hinson sec.

Brinn, John & Peggy Coale 28 Sept. 1814, Sam'l. Smith sec.
Brinn, Richard & Elizabeth Anderson 27 July 1793, Richard Sisson
    sec.
Brinn, William & Elizabeth Robinson 30 July 1819, John T.Oldham
    sec.

Brinnon, Benjamin & Maria Wheeler dau. Richard Wheeler, 31 Dec.
    1838, Levi Barnet sec.
Brinnon, Chilton & Elizabeth Sanford 15 Apr. 1829, Newman
    McKenney sec.
Brinnon, John & Elizabeth Crenshaw 25 Nov. 1799, John Norwood sec.
Brinnon, John & Elizabeth Steel dau. John B. Steel, 1 June 1813
    Benjamin L. Lale sec.
Brinnon, Owen & Elizabeth Palmer 26 Dec. 1814, Edward Spence sec.
Brinnon, William & Elizabeth Cash 27 Dec. 1820, Shilton Brinnon sec.
Brinnon, Youel & Sarah McKenney 27 Oct. 1792, William McKenney sec.

Brinham, William & Caty Moreton 3 Dec. 1805, James Ryals

Brimmer, Isaac & Margarett Young 27 Apr. 1798, Reubin Green sec.

Briant, George, son of Sarah Briant & Elizabeth Wright 5 Jan. 1835
    Richard P. Fones sec.

Briant, James & Venna J. Eskridge 21 Jan. 1830, John Briant sec.
Briant, James & Fanny Wroe 17 Dec. 1835, Richard Omohundro sec.
Briant, Jonathan & Sally Buckler 13 Feb. 1834, Martin Millmon sec.
Briant, Levi & Jane Codleen 29 Sept. 1804, Tarpley Briant sec.
Briant, Levi & Mary Harris 2 Jan. 1817, Tarpley Briant sec.
Briant, Levi & Mary Coats 9 Feb. 1828, Tarpley Briant sec.
Briant, Reuben & Nancy Iles 9 Oct. 1792, Frederick Weaver sec.
Briant, Reuben & Sally Mothershead 11 Mar. 1816, Nathaniel
    Mothershead sec.
Briant, Robert & Ann M. Marks 19 Feb. 1845 Henry Winkfield sec.

Briscoe, Reuben & Betsey Thorp 29 June 1790, Thomas Thorp sec.
Briscoe, Reubin & Ann B. Johnson, dau. Samuel Johnson, 19 Dec.
    1803, Joseph Fox, Jr. Sec.

Brook, Reuben & Ann Pierce dau. Randell Pierce, 10 Mar. 1825,
    Peter B. Dowdall sec.

Brockenbrough, Champ & Sally Skinker Bowie 24 Nov. 1795, John
    Peake sec.
Brockenbrough, Moore Fauntleroy & Sarah Ball 14 July 1817,
    Joseph Fox sec.

Bromley, Lewis B. & Louisa Winstead 12 Jan. 1831, Sam'l Bromley sec.

Brown, Christopher & Nancy Foxhall 28 July 1824,Tarpley Briant sec.
Brown, Christopher & Frances Marmaduke 22 Sept. 1825, George
    Coates sec.
Brown, Edwin & Harriet C. Johnson 9 Nov. 1839, William Edwards sec.
Brown, George F. & Martha F. Taliaferro 28 Nov. 1638, William A.
    Spence sec.
Browne, George H. & Mary E. S. Lyell 14 Dec. 1841, O.E.P. Hazard
    sec.
Brown, James T. & Polly Sandy 28 Dec. 1804
Brown, James & Ann Johnson 15 Feb. 1817, Thomas Palmer sec.
Brown, James & Elizabeth McKenney 26 Apr. 1825, Reuben McKenney sec.
Brown, John,Jr. & Ann Spence 15 Mar. 1794, Thomas Sandy sec.
Brown, John & Margaret Self 18 Sept. 1795, John C. Self sec.
Brown, John & Elizabeth Brown 21 Mar. 1801, Thomas Sutton sec.
Brown, John T. & Elizabeth Henage 21 Dec. 1813, Sam'l. B. Kelsick
    sec.
Brown, John & Jane Mullins 23 Aug. 1835, Sam'l. T. Reamy sec.
Brown, John & Sarah Sutton 2 Mar. 1837, Friar Sutton sec.
Brown, John & Susan Self 30 Jan. 1838, Peter L. Self sec.
Brown, Lemuel G. & Mariah Anton 3 Jan. 1848, William Suit sec.
Brown, Richard T. & Lucy Spark 27 Mar. 1806, Alexander Parker sec.
Brown, Richard & Sarah A. Watson, dau. George Watson, 28 Jan. 1838,
    John Sutton sec.
Brown, Thomas & Fanny Brown 8 Dec 1807, John Peake sec.
Brown, Thomas & Eliza Simpson 21 Dec. 1809, John W. Jones sec.
Brown, Thomas & Sarah S. Cox 3 July 1843, James S. Lvell sec.
Brown, William & Elizabeth Mullins 5 Nov. 1832, Chr Brown sec.
Brown, William W & Eleanor A. Costin 9 Apr. 1849, W. R. Sutton sec.

Bryan, Lovel & Elizabeth Weedon 7 Jan. 1793, Samuel Weedon sec.
Badly damaged.
Bryant, Charles & Mary Davis, dau. Jane Washington, 20 May 1845
George H. Sisson sec.
Bryant, George H. & Maria Brown 23 Dec. 1845, Christopher Brown sec.
Bryant, James & Catherine Brown 16 May 1848, Christopher Brown sec.
Bryant, John & Frances Brawner 28 Nov. 1796, James Bryant sec.
Bryant, John B. & Elizabeth Eskridge 29 Dec. 1831, Richard
Omohundro sec.
Bryant, Tarpley & Sarah Bariott, dau. John Bariott, 2 Apr. 1793
Reuben Bryant sec.
Bryant, Tarpley & Mary Kilman 6 Apr. 1836, William Tallent sec.

Bruer, Richard & Ann Blackwell 16 Oct. 1788, Thomas Spence sec.
Bruer, William & Magdalin Lewis, wid. 23 July 1793, Daniel
Harrison sec.

Bruce, Reuben & Martha Bayne 1 Feb. 1808, George Bruce sec.

Bulger, Edmund & Hannah Corbin Hudson 27 Mar. 1787, Thomas Caddeen
sec.
Bulger, Richard & Polly Jackson 7 June 1815, Richard Sanford sec.
Bulger, Thomas J. & Nancy Hall 15 Apr. 1812, Isaac Hall sec.
Bulger, William S. & Mary Brasshaw 4 Dec. 1819, Thomas J.Bulger sec.
Bulger, William L. & Frances Garner 24 Nov. 1834, Robert O.
Blakey sec.

Burkley, William & Susannah Muse 9 June 1806, John Butler sec.

Burrell, Spencer & Polly Hines 23 July 1825, John Clasbury sec.

Burton, Jesse & Susanna Burrell 27 Mar. 1828, Dan'l Harrison sec.

Burn, Edward & Milley Spurling 3 Apr. 1819, Henry Maskiel sec.
Burn, Edward & Nancy Carpenter 5 June 1797, Thomas Johnson sec.

Burgess, Daniel & Mary Wood 4 Mar. 1796, Samuel Smith sec.
Burgess, Harrison & Frances Wood 9 Oct. 1805, William Jett sec.
Burges, John, son of Joseph Burges, & Frances James Pitman 14 July
1792, Joseph Burgess sec.
Burgess, John & Nancy Benson 9 Oct. 1805, William Jett sec.
Burgess, William & Nancy Bragg 22 May 1815, Thomas M. Bragg sec.

Butler, Beckwith & Libby Ennis 26 Jan. 1829, Griffin R. Kirk sec.
Butler, Beckwith & Elizabeth Smoote 29 June 1829, Sam'l Davis sec.
Butler, Francis T.A. & Rebecca F. Brown 26 May 1845, Thomas T.
Beale sec.
Butler, George & Nelly Laycock 28 Mar. 1812, John Self sec.
Butler, James & Elizabeth Barecroft 31 Aug. 1790, Jeremiah
Rochaster sec.
Butler, James & Elizabeth Beale dau. Nancy Beale, wid., 12 Jan.
1796, John James Maund sec.
Butler, James B. & Elizabeth Parmer 23 July 1845, Randale Kirk sec.

Butler, Jesse & Sally Stott, dau. Robert Stott, 4 Dec. 1790
    William Butler sec.
Butler, John & ------ Shoots 24 Nov. 1786, Thomas Butler sec.
Butler, John & Mary Muse 4 Jan. 1796, William Williams sec.
Butler, Thomas & Frances Moxley 3 Dec 1787, Joseph Moxley,Jr. sec.
Butler, Thomas & Mary Maskiel, dau. Henry Maskiel, 22 Jan. 1834
    Richard Lyell sec.
Butler, Wesley & Frances T. Crask 24 Nov. 1813, George Quisenbury
    sec.
Butler, William & Alice Butler, dau. Christopher Butler, 11 Sept.
    1786, John Butler sec.
Butler, William & Amey Weston 16 July 1803, Daniel Sanford sec.
Butler, William & Polly Stoot 4 Feb. 1809, James Johnson sec.
Butler, William & Margaret Jacobs 15 Jan. 1814, John Potter sec.
Butler, William A. & Susan Fiffey 14 Dec. 1829, John Bayne sec.
Butler, William B. & Mary P. Harrison 14 Jan. 1834, James M.
    English sec.
Butler, William B. & Martha L. Gregory 2 Jan 1836, John Shackleford
    sec.
Butler, William B. & Maria Wilson 2 Dec. 1839, John Kirk sec.

Caddeen, Richard & Mary Bennett, wid. 3 Feb. 1787, Thomas Caddeen
    sec.

Calm, Charles & Martha Clarke dau. Elizabeth Crask, 25 June 1850
    E. Eliason sec.

Calvert, John M. & Caroline Betts 11 June 1849, David B. Taylor sec.

Callahan, Charles & Alice Hylard 6 June 1810
Callahan, William C. & Mary R. Rice 25 Mar. 1844, William H. Benson
    sec.

Campbell, John & Eliza Ferguson Murphy, dau. John Murphy, 7 Dec.
    1808, Samuel Lewis sec.

Cannaday, Reuben & Easter Green, wid. 24 Mar. 1789, Samuel Wood sec.

Carroll, John & Nancy Curtis 8 June 1822, George Curtis sec.
Carroll, John B. & Eliza Barnett 4 Nov. 1833, Levi Barnett sec.

Carr, John & Sarah Bruce 20 Jan. 1794, Joshua Boing sec.

Carter, Daniel & Nancy Fones 9 Sept. 1807, Thomas Coates sec.
Carter, Daniel & Sally Hinson 30 Oct. 1822, Daniel Carter sec.
Carter, George & Catherine B. Berkley, dau. William Berkley, 26
    Feb. 1834, William B. Sloughter sec.
Carter, George M. & Mary T. Rice 12 Dec. 1834, Thomas L. Muse sec.
Carter, John & Mary Carter 19 Sept. 1796, Elisha Newcomb sec.
Carter, John & Sary Brewer 15 Feb. 1798, James Brewer sec.
Carter, John S. & Eliza Ann Harrison 4 Mar. 1815, Thomas M.
    Bragg sec.

Carter, John S. & Ann Peirce 31 July 1824, Aaron Wallace sec.
Carter, Richard & Susannah Briscoe 21 Dec 1790, James Briscoe
   sec.
Carter, Robert & Nancy Spilman wid. 22 June 1795, Presley Neale sec.
Carter, Robert & Margaret Sanders 16 Feb. 1820, James Gutridge
   sec.
Carter, Tasker & Delia Reamy 29 Aug. 1825, Thomas Miller sec.

Carver, Richard H. & Amelia Bruce 27 Mar. 1826, Richard Bayne sec.

Cary, Cornelius & Elizabeth Jones 11 Nov. 1829, Edmund Tate sec.
Cary, George & Martha Brann 10 Jan. 1830, Job Self sec.
Cary, Newton & Ann Gallagher 18 June 1825, Henry Beale, Jr. sec.
Cary, Thomas & Rachel Newman 24 May 1848, Cephus Newman sec.
Carey, George Barnwell & Winifred Garner, dau. Jane Garner, 16
   July, 1794, Stephen Crane sec.
Carey, George & Ann Gaskins 2 Sept. 1641, William Read sec.
Carey, John, son of George B. Carey, & Jane Elmore 5 Nov. 1831
   Thomas Parks sec.
Carey, Stafford & Judy Gaskins 29 Nov. 1842, Thomas Carey sec.
Carey, Vanness & Frances Ann Johnson 28 Dec. 1847, Frederick
   Newman sec.
Carey, William & Julia Ann Holliday, dau. Fielding Holliday,
   23 Mar. 1836, John B. Olive sec.

Carpenter, Alexander & Mary Jane Miller 28 Jan. 1850, Washington
   Bayne sec.
Carpenter, James & Susanna Bland 7 Mar. 1808, John Carpenter sec.
Carpenter, Jeremiah & Nancy Oliff 20 Mar. 1817, Dan'l Carter sec.
Carpenter, John & Nancy Reamy 13 Feb. 1818, Jacob A. Reamy sec.
Carpenter, Joseph & Shady Hinson 7 Mar. 1849, Frederick Poor sec.
Carpenter, Meredith & Jane Sanders 23 Dec. 1815, Aleck Sanders sec.
Carpenter, Samuel & Malinda Spurling 9 Jan. 1821, Elisha Spurling
   sec.
Carpenter, William & Mary Cavender 31 Dec. 1806, James Montgomery
   sec.
Carpenter, William & Catherine Brewer 7 Jan. 1818, Joshua Reamey
   sec.
Carpenter, William & Mary Pope 20 Jan. 1824, William M. Crabb sec.

Cash, John & Rebecca Jones 27 Mar. 1848, Edwin G. Reed sec.

Cavender, Dozier T. & Elizabeth Gill 14 June 1793, George Cavender
   sec.
Cavender, Thomas & Sarah Scinner 16 May 1809, Samuel Gilbert sec.

Chasbury, John & Nancy Fryer 23 July 1825, Spencer Burrell sec.

Chandler, Hanibal & Lucy P. Bowcock, dau. Henry Bowcock, 20 May
   1842, Thomas Jett Redmon sec.
Chandler, William C. & Sally R. Crabb 23 Nov. 1807, William P.
   Crabb sec.
Chandler, William C. & Susan Mongar 6 Jan. 1821, Smith Dozier sec.

Chastain, Lewis & Elizabeth Rust, wid., 23 July 1793, John
    Brinnon sec.

Chambers, Thomas & Patsy Astin 8 Jan. 1827, Rodham Astin sec.

Chilton, Orrick & Felicia Corbin 19 Dec. 1791, Alexander Parker
    sec.

Chilley, Moses & Frances Sutton, wid. 15 Mar. 1837, Isaac A. Newton
    sec.
                Catherine
Chowning, Robert H. &/Rebecca Bowie, dau. Walter Bowie, 11 Apr.
    1835, William Huet sec.

Chrisman, Charles & Bethlehem Rose 12 May 1792, John Marmaduke sec.

Christopher, George & Ann Beale 18 July 1803, John Peake sec.

Claughton, Pemberton & Sally Neale 3 Sept. 1796, William Claughton
    sec.
Claughton, Peter C. & Hannah R. Lamkin 26 Nov. 1824, James C.
    Wright sec.

Clapham, Josias & Hannah West Hodge 22 July 1822, John Campbell
    sec.

Claybrook, Robert & Charlotte Brown 5 Aug. 1839, J.L.Bailey sec.

Clanahan, John M. & Mary Robinson, dau. Solomon Robinson, 27 Dec.
    1791, Solomon Robinson sec.

Claxton, Jeremiah & Molly Payton 9 Sept. 1786, Anthony Payton sec.
Claxton, Jeremiah & Frances Sanford 23 Mar. 1799
Claxton, Thomas & Alice Weaver, sister of Susanna Weaver, 17 Jan.
    1798, George Deatterly sec.

Clark, James & Penelope Sanford dau. Reuben Sanford, 28 May. 1796
    John Grinnan sec.
Clark, James H. & Elizabeth W. Riley 17 Dec. 1829, Gerard A.
    Sanford sec.
Clark, Richard & Sarah Cooper 27 Mar. 1792, William Butler sec.
Clark, Richard & Sally B. Smith, dau. Peter Smith, 23 May 1814,
    James S. Smith sec.
Clark, Thomas & Jimima Scutt 10 Oct. 1787, John Griggs sec.
Clark, Thomas William & Frances Wrow 21 Dec. 1797, William Riley sec.
Clark, Thomas W. & Frances Sanford 25 Sept. 1848, John F. Bispham
    sec.

Clarke, Henry & Susan Davis 9 Jan 1834, William J. Sanford sec.
Clarke, Richard & Elizabeth Hallbrooks -- Dec. 1819, Elliott Stone
    sec.
Clarke, Richard H. & Cornelia Johnson 15 Dec. 1842, Mathias Johnson
    sec.
Clarke, Thomas & Eliza Burch 17 June 1817, John Sanford sec.

Clarke, Thomas W. & Susan Sanford dau. William S. Sanford, 31 Aug.
    1830, James Crask sec.

Cleaves, Thomas H. & Emeline Van Ness 16 July 1841, Benjamin Van
    Ness sec.

Coats, George & Peggy McKenny 19 Oct. 1809, Tarply Bryant sec.
Coats, James & Elizabeth Carpenter (not dated) bundle marked
    "1812" John Carter sec.
Coats, James, Jr. & Nancy R. Carpenter 12 Jan. 1825, James Coats
    sec.
Coats, James & Delila P. Fones 15 Sept. 1828, James Reamey sec.
Coats, James & Martha Ann Gutridge, dau. Frances Morris, 28 Dec.
    1846, Henry R. Gutridge sec.
Coats, Joseph & Nancy Sanford 27 Dec. 1815, William Carpenter sec.
Coats, William & Franky Carpenter 4 Nov. 1807, Daniel Carter sec.

Coates, George & Polly Spark 6 Jan. 1825, Thomas M. Jenkins sec.
Coates, John A. & Elizabeth Balderson 19 Nov. 1833, Samuel Coates
    sec.
Coates, Richard S. & Patty Hart 7 Jan. 1834, Fenner Carter sec.

Cahoon, Andrew & Prissilley Weaver 5 Aug. 1790, Elijah Weaver sec.

Colvin, William Furlong & Agathy Wright 8 Nov. 1792, John Barker
    sec.

Cole, George W. & Mary M. Sandford 28 Dec. 1842, Richard R.King sec
Cole, Thomas M. W. & Mary A. Spence 22 May 1844, Edward B.
    Omohundro sec.
Cole, William & Jane E. McClanahan 29 Mar. 1826, Hiram S. King sec.

Colebuck, Thomas & Matilda Garner 19 Dec 1788, John Garner sec.

Coleman, John & Susanna Critcher 18 Jan. 1788, John Critcher sec.
Coleman, Richard & Mary Moore 23 Dec. 1824, Griffin R. Kirk sec.
Coleman, Thomas & Hannah Boyer 18 Dec. 1792, Daniel Boyer sec.

Collins, Christopher J. & Elizabeth Washington Lindrum dau Thomas
    Lindrum 21 Apr. 1806, Joseph Fox sec.
Collins, Christopher & Fanny Peirce 3 Mar. 1807, Samuel Templeman
    sec.
Collins, James & Priscilla McCay 14 Jan. 1823, Walter Mann sec.

Coloson, Peter & Susan Simms 11 Jan. 1811, Richard H. Simms sec.

Collison, Peter & Mariah Johnson 13 May 1819, George Johnson sec.

Colliston, William & Kessey Johnson 15 Oct. 1804, Thomas Johnson sec

Collinsworth, Catesby & Mary Jeffery 10 Aug. 1823, J.F.Harvey sec.
Collinsworth, John & Sebinah Weaver 3 June 1790, John Brown Steal se
Collinsworth, John & Fanny Collinsworth 28 Mar. 1811, Samuel C.
    Annandale sec.

Collinsworth, Nathaniel & Nancy Garner 2 Dec. 1797, Linsey Cole
    sec. Badly damaged
Collinsworth, William & Nancy Caddeau 26 Oct. 1789, John Butler sec.
Collinsworth, William W. T. & Martha R. Self 7 Apr. 1827, William
    Barnett sec.

Compton, Alexander & Felicia Beale 8 Nov. 1836, Sam'l B. Atwill sec.

Combs, Thomas E. D. & Ann Dodd 31 Dec. 1822

Connellee, Autumn & Elizabeth R. Hardwick 31 Dec. 1839, Gilchrist
    Connellee sec.
Connellee, Gilchrist & Eliza Worney 1 Jan. 1849, W. R. Sutton sec.
Connelle, James D. & Mary W. McKenny dau. Reubin McKenny, 10 Sept.
    1829, James Scales sec.
Connellee, James P. & Martha C. Edmonds 10 Jan. 1849, Theodoric
    N. Balderson sec.
Connellee, John T. & Mary S. Rose, dau. Bennett Rose, 15 Dec. 1835
    William H. Reynolds sec.
Connollee, Robert C. & Lucy Hazard 14 Jan. 1817, William Mothers-
    head sec.
Connally, Thornton & Betsy S. Acred 16 June 1814, John R. McGuire
    sec.

Cooper, George & Sarah Wills 9 Dec. 1801 (bond signed but not
    filled in)

Cook, John & Ann Barrott 12 Dec. 1842, James Edmunds sec.
Cook, Samuel & Maria Dekins dau. James Dekins, 2 Nov. 1830,
    Meredith Lucas sec.
Cook, Thomas, Jr. & Sally Hullums 23 Nov. 1791, Thomas Cook sec.

Cooke, Austin & Elizabeth Ann Mothershead 2 Sept. 1833, William L.
    Mothershead sec.
Cooke, Henry & Ailcy Jenkins 17 Sept. 1828, John Massey sec.
Cooke, James Steward & Sarah Edmonds 13 Apr. 1800, James Edmonds sec.
Cooke, Steward & Eliza Hinson 25 Apr. 1833, Meredith Lucas sec.

Corbin, John B. & Elizabeth M. Hutt, dau. Gerard Hutt, 24 Nov. 1828
    S. S. Hutt sec.

Cotterell, Lionel J. & Fanny D. Oliff, 2 Apr. 1821, James Pratt sec.

Courtney, Benjamin & Mary Smith - Consent of Jeremiah Smith dated
    27 Aug. 1801, witnessed by Jeremiah Jeffries
Courtney, David C. & Eliza Ann Smith 15 Feb. 1847, James R.
    Courtney sec.
Courtney, George & Ann Jeffries, dau. William D. Jeffries, 2 Jan.
    1787, James Courtney sec.
Courtney, George & Hannah Rice 6 Aug. 1805, John Crenshaw sec.
Courtney, George & Elizabeth A. Branson 27 May 1850, John M.
    Branson sec.
Courtney, James R. & Mary R. Sutton 6 Jan. 1848, R. W. Yeatman
    sec.

Courtney, Jeremiah & Lydia A. Courtney, dau. W. J. Courtney, 17
    May 1836, Mathew R. King sec.
Courtney, John & Elizabeth Mors 27 Dec. 1791, Jeremiah Garner sec.
Courtney, John H. & Sally Palmer 13 Apr. 1831, George Brown sec.
Courtney, Linsey & Caty Garner - Consent of Caty Garner dated --
    1803, Witnessed by Jeremiah Jeffries - Bond signed but
    not filled in - Jeremiah Jeffries sec.
Courtney, Malachi & Mary Brown 15 Aug. 1826, William Courtney sec.
Courtney, Robert B. & Nancy Carvin 22 June 1809, George Smith sec.
Courtney, William & Nancy Crenshaw - Consent of Nancy Crenshaw
    dated 22 Mar. 1813, Witnessed by John Crenshaw
Courtney, William J. & Elizabeth B. Lamkin 3 July 1834, John
    English sec.

Covington, Thomas D. & Mary R. Stowers dau. Thomas Stowers - Con-
    sent of Thomas Stowers dated 29 Mar. 1813

Cowart, John & Elizabeth Redman 23 Jan. 1806, Fredrick Anderson sec.

Cox, Downing & Eliza M. Sisson 21 Dec. 1818, Richard J. Thompson
    & Elliott S. Minor sec.
Cox, Fleet & Sarah H. Murphy, dau. John Murphy 28 June 1822, M.M.
    Marmaduke sec.
Cox, James & Hannah Jackson 12 June 1804, John Watt sec.
Cox, John & Mary W. Hipkins, dau. Robert S. Hipkins 16 Dec. 1826
    Frederick Jones sec.
Cox, Peter P. & Fanny Bailey 18 Oct. 1796, Fleet Cox sec.
Cox, Peter P. & Sally Gordon 16 June 1802, Ransdell Peirse sec.
Cox, Peter P. & Eleonor Jackson 17 Aug. 1808, James Elliott sec.
Cox, Peter P. & Ann M. Leland 6 Sept. 1834, Edward Cox sec.
Cox, Presley & Sally Ricarda Lee 8 June 1815, Henry Hungerford sec.

Craine, Stephen & Clay Hewlet 2 Jan. 1793, Jeremiah Garner sec.

Crabb, Daniel & Frances Burgess Smith, dau. Sampson Smith --1789
Crabb, Daniel & Frances Middleton 3 Oct. 1789, Ashton Lamkin sec.
Crabb, Daniel, Sr. & Ann Gill 24 Aug. 1795, Newyear Branson sec.
Crabb, Ozmond & Winifred Hartly 7 Jan. 1790, John Mezzeck sec.
Crabb, Ro: H. P. & Jane F. Walker 1 Jan. 1838, James English sec.
Crabb, Samuel & Mary Middleton 27 Aug. 1793, Charles Thompson sec.
Crabb, Sturman & Mary E. Dozier 25 May 1843, William A. Spence sec.
Crabb, William M. & Sally Lee Randolph 19 Dec. 1809, Philip J. A.
    Crabb sec.
Crabb, William P. & Eliza Ann Yeatman, dau. Ann H. Yeatman, 7 Nov.
    1827, G. G. Mothershead sec.

Craighill, John & Elizabeth Hipkins 31 Oct. 1786, Thomas Streshly
    sec.
Craghill, William & Charlott Hipkins 30 Apr. 1787, Thomas
    Streschley sec.
Crask, James & Elizabeth Bragg 17 Mar. 1819, James Rowles sec.
Crask, James & Ann Sanford 12 July 1827, William Sutton sec.
Crask, John & Shady Carpenter dau. John Carpenter, 23 Dec. 1808,
    James Peed sec. Badly damaged.

Crask, Marks & Mary Payne 12 Dec. 1808, Thomas Omohundro sec.
Crask, Marks & Caty Collins 1 Jan. 1810, William Doleman sec.
Crask, Richard & Frances B. Doleman 19 Nov. 1818, Henry A.
    Riley sec.
Crask, William & Frances Jenkins 14 Nov. 1786, Richard McGinniss
    sec.
Crask, William H. & Mary Yeatman 8 Jan. 1845, Williamson Hall sec.

Crenshaw, John & Betsy Norwood 11 Dec. 1813, Richard Croxton sec.

Cridlin, Burton & Emily Owens 23 July 1832, Sam'l Dishman sec.
Cridlin, Burton & Nancy Carpenter 24 June 1844, Frederick Poor sec.
Cridlin, W. Nelson, overseer of Baldwin M. Lee, & Nancy White, dau.
    William White - Consent of William White dated 2 Feb.
    1802, Witnessed by Charles Wickliff & Nathaniel King
Cridlin, William & Ailcey Reade 10 Nov. 1823, John Peade sec.

Crismond, John B. & Sally Ryalls 23 Apr. 1823, Bethell Tallent sec.
Crismond, John B. & Polly Weaver 11 Nov. 1830, James Carpenter sec.

Critcher, George & Elizabeth D. Palmer 25 Nov. 1839, R. S.
    Mickleborough sec.
Critcher, John & Lettice Garner 22 June 1792, George T. Lee sec.

Croxton, Thomas & Elizabeth B. Spence 13 Nov. 1806, William M.
    Walker sec.

Curtis, George & Molly Douglass 12 Feb. 1794, Gerard Gardner sec.
Curtis, George & Nancy Doleman 27 Apr. 1801, Rodham Hudson sec.
Curtis, John B. & Sarah T. Woosoncroft 23 Aug. 1824, William
    Hazard sec.

Dade, Isaac & Fanny Blundell 18 Dec. 1786, James Peirce sec.

Daffron, Vincent D. & Sarah Doleman 23 June 1801, John Codde,
    Richard Clarke & G. McKinney sec.

Daingerfield, LeRoy & Elizabeth Parker dau. Richard Parker, 17
    Oct. 1786, Henry S. Redman sec.
Daingerfield, LeRoy P. & Juliet O. Parker, dau. William H. Parker
    sec.

Dakins, Middleton & Alcy Lucass 21 Nov. 1826, Henry Winkfield sec.

Damron, Fleet & Polly Garner 22 Jan. 1821, Jeremiah Gawn sec.

Dameron, Willis & Jemima Rice 6 Nov. 1817, Thomas Taylor sec.
Dameron, William M. & Jemima Spence 20 Dec. 1827, Joseph D.
    Slocum sec.

Danks, George B. & Priscilla Pritchett 28 Oct. 1805, Newman
    Jackson sec.
Danks, George B. & Mary Cane 26 Apr. 1824, George Curtis sec.
Dank, John & Nancy Gilbert (not dated - Bundle marked "1801")
    Bond signed but not filled in - William Porter sec.

Daniel, George & Hannah King 18 Nov. 1795, William Middleton sec.

Daniel, George & Magdalen Williams 4 Oct. 1815, William King sec.

Darnaby, William & Margaret N. Berkley, dau. William Berkley, 14
    May 1827, Charles W. Payton sec.

Davis, Addison J. & Mary Coats 29 Oct. 1841

Davis, George & Sally Billings 5 July 1826, James Ferguson sec.

Davis, James & Ellen Hall 20 Aug. 1821, William McGuire sec.

Davis, James & Elizabeth Bunyan 22 Sept. 1825, Thomas Oharrow sec.

Davis, John & Amiss, Griffis 13 Dec. 1786, Thomas Butler sec.

Davis, John & Betsy Dolman, dau. William Dolman, dec. 22 Jan.
    1796, James McNeil sec.

Davis, John & Elizabeth Lacy 5 Dec. 1807, David Goldsby sec.

Davis, John & Harriet Poor 21 Feb. 1834, Frederick Poor sec.

Davis, Joseph & Martha F. Beale, dau. Robert Beale, 28 Sept. 1833
    Robert Beale, Jr. sec.

Davis, Joseph W. L. & Ann E. Sanford 20 Jan. 1846, William Wroe
    sec.

Davis, Peter & Polly McGuire 14 Sept. 1792, George McKenny sec.

Davis, Peter & Elizabeth Shirly - Consent (not signed) dated 29
    July 1813 - No witness - Bond signed but not filled in.

Davis, Samuel & Fanny Smith 16 Dec. 1806, Sisson McKenney sec.

Davis, Samuel & Fanny Luttrell 2 Nov. 1816, Simon Robinson sec.

Davis, Samuel & Nancy Weaver 8 Mar. 1827, Henry Weaver sec.

Davis, Samuel & Ann Quisenbury 18 Mar. 1835, Nicholas Quisenbury
    sec.

Davis, Thomas & Sally Drake, dau. Rose Drake, Consent of Rose Drake
    (not dated - in bundle marked "1799") bond signed but not
    filled in - George ------ sec. Badly damaged.

Davis, Thomas S. & Eliza Davis, dau. Elizabeth Davis, 11 July 1814
    William Settle sec.

Davis, Thomas S. & Mary Elizabeth Field 6 Feb. 1819, Thomas Wright
    sec.

Davis, Thomas L. & Ann Robinson 8 Feb. 1832, Newman McKenney sec.

Davis, William & Anne Worth 15 Feb. 1791, Thomas Worth sec.

Davis, William L. & Elizabeth H. King 27 Jan. 1794, William H.
    King sec.

Davis, William H. & Saly Curtis, Consent of Saly Curtis dated 25
    May 1822, witnessed by J. L. Mullins - Bond signed but
    not filled in - Catesby------- sec.

Davis, William & Margaret Davis 3 July 1828, Samuel Davis sec.

Davis, William & Elizabeth H. Beale, dau. Robert Beale, Sr., 20
    Dec. 1837, Robert Beale, Jr. sec.

Davis, Youell & Caty Preits 29 Dec. 1795, James Rowls sec.

Davis, Youell & Susanna Pecure (sic) Consent of Susanna Pecure
    dated 28 Aug. 1821, Bond signed but not filled in.

Day, Samuel & Lotty Ashton 7 Jan. 1818, Samuel Tate sec.

Deane, James & Leanna Washington 8 Dec. 1808, Rodham Hinson sec.

Deatley, George & Sally Mothershead 22 Sept. 1789, Humphrey Pope
    sec.

Deatly, George & Lucinda Alton 24 Dec. 1805, Thomas Bett--worth
 sec. Damaged.
Deatley, Henry & Sally Tate 9 Aug. 1804, Henry Washington sec.
Deatly, Mathew & Maria Mitchell 29 Dec. 1820, William Deatly sec.
Deatley, Meredith & Lucinda Weaver 14 Jan. 1824, Vincent Moore sec.
Deatley, Richard B. & Elizabeth Berkley, dau. William Berkley,
 13 Sept. 1844, W. G. Walker sec.
Deatley, William & Ellen Briscoe 2 Mar. 1801, Christopher Deatley
 sec.
Deatley, William & Susanner Winsterd 28 Mar. 1818, William Deatley
 sec.

Deaterly, James & Elizabeth Fegitt 22 Mar. 1788, John Sanders sec.

Deakins, John & Elizabeth Teete, 31 Dec. 1822, Walker Winkfield sec.
Deakins, Middleton & Catherine Edmunds 29 Dec. 1829, Meredith Lucas
 sec.
Decons, John & Lucy Washington 2 Dec. 1847, Joseph Mozingo sec.

Delano, Darius & Betsey How 22 Aug. 1827, George Delano sec.

Dement, George & Elizabeth Harrison 31 Jan. 1827, William Gilbert
 sec.

Denney, Edmund & Betsey Triplett 18 Nov. 1791, William Triplett sec.

Dick, Young & Judith Tate 3 June 1805 John Watts & Jesse Tate sec.

Dishman, Charles & Eliza T. Smith dau. Betsy Smith, 6 Sept. 1830
 John T. Smith sec.
Dishman, James & Amanda McDaniel 8 June 1829, Charles Dishman sec.
Dishman, James & Ann V. Kent 31 Oct. 1836, Thomas Sandy sec.
Dishman, John & Mary McDaniel, dau. Mary Simms, 18 Jan. 1830,
 John Hunter sec.
Dishman, William & Elizabeth Morrel 27 Dec. 1786, William Morrel sec.
Dishman, William & Elizabeth White 1 Mar. 1810, William White sec.

Ditty, Thomas R. & Eliza A. Payne, neice of D. Payne, 14 Apr. 1835
 James H. Payne sec.

Dixon, James B. & Elizabeth R. Coghill 17 July 1820, William
 Coghill sec.
Dixon, William & Judy Harrison 6 Dec. 1847, Charles C. Baker sec.

Dodd, Alexander & Margarett Griffin 12 July 1821, Samuel Mothershead
 sec.
Dodd, James & Patty Massey, Dau. Elizabeth Massey, 2 Nov. 1790,
 James Dodd sec.
Dodd, Joseph & Elizabeth Bryant 5 Mar. 1810, James Mothershead sec.
Dodd, John & Elizabeth Sanford 24 Dec. 1791, John Brawner sec.
Dodd, Joseph & Elizabeth Mothershead 8 Nov. 1815, George G.
 Mothershead sec.
Dodd, William & Henrietta Weaver 2 Mar. 1787, Richard Weaver sec.

Doleman, Jacob V. & Mary M. Jenkins 24 Dec. 1829, James P. Jenkins
sec.
Doleman, John H. & Frances Bavne Vigar 10 June 1805, John Davis
sec.
Doleman, Thomas & Sally Hazzard 23 Jan. 1809, John H. Doleman sec.
Doleman, William & Ammaly Montgomery 14 Dec. 1796, James Montgomery
sec.

Donehow, James & Elender Fones 4 Apr. 1805, James Sutton sec.

Donnahaw, Richard H. & Sarah A. Thrift, dau. Jeremiah Thrift, 8
Nov. 1843, Samuel R. Thrift sec.

Dotley, William & Lucinda Deatley, dau. Christopher Deatley, 12
Aug. 1815, Meredith Deatley sec.

Douglass, Henry & Mary Harte 7 July 1842, George W. H. Reamy sec.
Douglass, Lemuel & Sarah Palmer 30 Dec. 1841, Joseph H. Moone sec.
Douglass, Rodham & Ellen P. Hardwick 10 Dec. 1829, Daniel Hardwick
sec.
Douglass, Rodham & Mary France 29 July 1837, Richard Hogan sec.
Douglass, Thomas H. & Maria Spurling - Not dated - in bundle
marked "1815"
Douglass, Thomas & Nancy S. Johnson 11 Nov. 1819, Patrick S.
Sanford sec.
Douglas, Vincent & Hanna King 14 Feb. 1814, William King sec.
Douglass, Vincent & Elizabeth Self 7 Feb. 1827, John Anton sec.

Downing, Thomas D. & Betsey Cox, 17 Mar. 1787, Fleet Cox,Jr. sec.

Dozier, Allen L. & Nancy Shackleford, dau. Elizabeth Dozier & dau.
in law of William R. Dozier, 9 July 1810, Vincent Dozier
sec.
Dozier, Austin & Elizabeth Dozier 23 Mar. 1831, Fryar Sutton sec.
Dozier, James & Betsy Muse, dau. Thomas Muse, 5 Feb. 1805, Richard
T. Brown & William Rice sec.
Dozier, Joseph & Sally Muse 16 Sept. 1811, John Pursley sec.
Dozier, Martin & Nancy Wilson 15 Feb. 1825, Ishmael Bragg sec.
Dozier, Martin & Elizabeth Butler 9 Feb. 1827, William Sutton sec.
Dozier, Nelson R. & Sophia T. Arnest 10 Jan. 1838, William R.
Dozier sec.
Dozier, Richard & Ann Rebecca Carroll 19 Dec. 1848, Benjamin Short
sec.
Dozier, Thomas & Frances Jones 13 Jan. 1808, Samuel Templeman sec.
Dozier, Vincent & Susan Smith (not dated - in bundle marked "1811")
James Dozier sec.

Drake, Benjamin & Rachel Hall 9 Nov. 1849, Martin Killmon sec.
Drake, Corbin & Lettis Gawen 7 Mar. 1829, William King sec.
Drake, Henry & Nancy Reamy 2 Mar. 1818, James Reamy sec.
Drake, James & Jenny Jones 2 Jan. 1793, William Roe sec.
Drake, John & Mary Ann Green 5 Dec. 1838, George Green sec.
Drake, Newton & Margaret James 26 Jan. 1829, George Barrock sec.
Drake, Rodham & Elizabeth Owens 8 Apr. 1839, John Drake sec.

Drake, Richard & Jane Thomson, dau. John Thomson, 21 Jan. 1787,
William Ryals sec.
Drake, Richard F. & Nancy Edmons 30 Nov. 1818, Thomas Sanders sec.
Drake, William & Ann Payton, dau. Margaret Butler, 15 Sept. 1789
John Drake sec.

Dunlop, George & Lucy Mahorny dau. Thomas Mahorny, 23 Dec. 1846,
Daniel G. Mahorney sec.

Dunahaw, John & Jemima McKenney 18 Nov. 1829, Richard McKenney sec.
Dunahaw, John H. & Charlott E. Barber 25 Sept. 1845, James R.
Barber sec.
Dunnahaw, William H. & Margaret A. Smith, dau. William Smith, 20
Dec. 1842, Conaway Reynolds sec.

Duvall, Howard M. & Juliet M. Davis 15 Oct. 1838, William Hutt sec.

Edmons, William & Alcey Short - Consent of Alcey Short dated 29
Oct. 1832, Witnessed by Uriah E. Head.

Edmonds, James & Margaret Lucus 6 Feb. 1815, Jeremiah Edmonds sec.
Edmonds, James & Alice Cook 21 Nov. 1822, John Massey sec.
Edmonds, Jeremiah & Martha Carter 2 Apr. 1791, Nathaniel Mothershead
sec.
Edmonds, Jeremiah & Molly Harris 13 Feb. 1803, Vincent Edmonds sec.
Edmonds, Meredith M. & Mary B. Canthorn 1 Feb. 1821, Vincent
Edmonds sec.
Edmonds, Richard & Penelope Marks 3 Jan. 1820, Campbell Teet sec.
Edmonds, Vincent & Frances Balderson 16 June 1798, Gilbert
Balderson sec.
Edmonds, William & Alcy Short 29 Oct. 1832, Uriah E. Head sec.

Edmunds, James & Molly Cook 3 Dec. 1788, Thomas Cook sec.

Edwards, Richard & Ann Maria McKinney, dau. Gerard McKinney, 22 Jan.
1829, Gerard McKinney sec.
Edwards, Thomas & Elizabeth S. Templeman 17 Oct. 1817, Samuel
Templeman, Jr. sec.
Edwards, Thomas W. & Mary D. Jones 5 May 1848, James Gregory sec.
Edwards, Rev. William & Frankey Pope 3 Dec. 1790, Edward Porter sec.
Edwards, William & Sarah N. Taylor 26 June 1826, Robert Bailey sec.
Edwards, William & Clarissa A. R. Crabb 18 Dec. 1844, S. B. Atwill
sec.

Efford, Samuel & Elizabeth Doleman 16 Dec. 1793, John Doleman sec.

Eidson, James & Susannah Nash 21 Dec. 1825, John Spilman sec.

Eliff, Henry & Frances Stone, dau. Alice Stone, 28 Feb. 1824,
William Bulger sec.

Ellis, Richard L. & Emily H. Douglass, dau. James Douglass, 30 Nov.
1818, William Nelson sec.

Elliot, Rev. James & Elizabeth Brockenbrough dau. Arthur Brockenbrough, 20 Nov. 1792, James Bland sec.

Ellmore, John & ------lander Cluskey 17---- 1787, Ebenezer Morse
sec. Badly damaged.
Elmore, Edmund T. K. & Mary Barnett 16 Aug. 1841, John B. Carroll
sec.
Elmore, Griffin & Elizabeth Beale dau. Henry Beale, Sr., 18 Feb.
1825, Henry Beale Jr. sec.
Elmore, John, Jr. & Nancy Hall 4 Dec. 1798, John Elmore, Sr. sec.
Elmore, John H. & Lucy Jane Edwards 11 Dec. 1826, William Edwards
sec.
Elmore, John, Sr. & Lucy Hillyard 9 Nov. 1829, Enoch G. Jeffries sec
Elmore, John & Ann B. Jeffries 7 June 1844, Robert Murphy sec.

Eniss, William & Margaret Brinn, consent of Margaret Brinn dated
10 Feb. 1802, Witnessed by John Gregorey.
Ennis, Thomas & Caty Carpenter 18 June 1796, Youel Brinnon sec.
Ennis, William & Jane McKenney 14 Apr. 1845, Fleet B. Anton sec.

English, Benjamin S. & Mary F. Smith 18 Jan. 1841, Moses Chilley sec
English, James W. & Eliza Courtney 19 Dec. 1832, Mathew R. King sec
English, John & Letty A. Rice 16 Dec. 1833, William T. Branson sec.
English, Samuel W. & Sarah Ann Delano 23 Dec. 1844, Benedict Walker
sec.

Ensco, Edward & Elizabeth Burgess 13 July 1808, Dan'l. Burgess sec.

Eskridge, Birdett & Ann Washington 31 Dec. 1800, Thomas Omohundro
sec.
Eskridge, Burrel S. & Elizabeth Kilmon 14 May 1829, Tarpley Bryant
sec.
Eskridge, John & Elizabeth Moxley 9 Dec. 1799, Rodham Moxley sec.
Eskridge, Richard & Ann Good 11 Jan. 1825, Meredith Lucas sec.
Eskridge, Thomas & Winefred Byles 13 Feb. 1797, Rodham Moxley sec.

Eubank, Thomas N. & Ann E. Nelson 23 May 1842, David H. Tapscott
sec.

Evins, John & Judy Tate 28 Apr. 1795, Hugh Quinton sec.

Fairfax, Dr. Ferdinando & Mary Ann Piper Jett 10 Jan. 1831, Joseph
L. Lyell sec.

Fauntleroy, Henry & Ann S. Sisson 16 Oct. 1828, Edward Spence sec.

Fegens, James & Molly Self 29 Sept. 1787, William Habron sec.

Feagitt, John & Caty Self 21 May 1794, Presley Self sec.
Feggitt, James & Molley Jones, dau. William Jones, 2 Dec. 1789
William Jones sec.
Feggitt, John & Nancey Mullins 14 June 1790, Thomas Gregory sec.

23

Figot, John & Nancey Mullins - Consent of Nancey Mullins dated
    13 June 1790, Witnessed by Thomas Gregory.
Piggot, Thomas & Matilday Colebock 30 Aug. 1793, Jesse Butler sec.

Figget, James & Hannah McKenny 22 Dec. 1800, Henry McKenny sec.
Figget, Spencer & Mary Dodd, dau. Joseph Dodd, 3 Oct. 1801,
    Berryman Dodd sec.

Fergusson, Robert & Elizabeth Ballantine, dau. John Ballantine,
    20 May 1787, Beckwith Butler sec.

Finch, Enock & Elizabeth Muse Moxly, 21 Dec. 1807, Richard
    Efford sec.

Fisher, William H. & Sally B. Spurling 20 Jan. 1829, Joseph
    Hazard sec.

Fitzhugh, Bolling & Fanny Fitzhugh, dau. George Fitzhugh, 29 Dec.
    1807, Daniel Carmichael sec.
Fitzhugh, Dr. George & Lucy Stuart, dau. in law of George
    Fitzhugh - Consent of George Fitzhugh dated 26 Sept. 1803
    Ink spilled on bond - Illegible - Joseph Fox, Jr. sec.

Fones, Charles & Elinor Muse 10 Feb. 1807, Thomas Coats sec.
Fones, Hampton M. & Margaret Ann Oatis, dau. William Oatis,
    9 Jan. 1845, William B. Butler sec.
Fones, James B. & Mary Ann Gutridge 19 Dec. 1833, Richard C.
    Gutridge sec.
Fones, James M. & Maria Bartlett 29 Sept. 1836, Samuel R. Fones
    sec.
Fones, James M. & Elizabeth Jackson 18 Aug. 1838, George H.
    Sisson sec.
Fones, James & Martha Brown 11 Aug. 1842, Richard G. Gutridge sec.
Fones, Samuel R. & Nancy Wilson 26 Oct. 1815, William Sanders sec.
Fones, William T. & Frances F. Jenkins 17 Mar. 1846, Thomas B.
    Spence sec.

Foorde, George & Nancy Poosy 17 June 1807, Armstrong McKenny sec.

Forbes, Gordon & Mary M. Harrington 17 Mar. 1835, William Hutt
    sec.
Forbos, William & Hannah Gordon 30 Dec. 1795, James Bland sec.

Fowke, Thomas & Susanna Baker, 26 May 1814, Joseph Fox sec.

Fox, Joseph & Mary Hipkins 5 Apr. 1788, John Marmaduke sec.

Foxall, Daniel & Sibbiner Lawrence 11 Oct. 1815, John Grinan sec.

Frank, Brodrington & Mary Beane 31 Aug. 1795

Franks, Henry & Franky Sanford 27 Feb. 1797, Eppa Weathers sec.
Franks, William & Elizabeth Sanford 31 Jan. 1787, James Friggitt
    sec.

Francis, Nash & Frances L. Bailey 1 Feb. 1847, William Baily sec.

Franklin, Thomas & Nancy Hall 27 Dec. 1810, William H. Hall sec.
Franklin, Thomas & Harriet Sutton, 9 Feb. 1814, Friar Sutton sec.
Franklin, William & Ann Collinsworth 30 Oct. 1786, John Collins-
    worth sec.
Franklin, William & Nancy White 28 Jan. 1805, James Sutton sec.
Franklin, Zachariah & Lucy Hinson 2 Feb. 1825, William Tallent sec.

Fryer, Samuel & Haney Ennis 1 Sept. 1804, Thomas Ennis sec.

Fulks, John B. & Nancy Mozengo, dau. Sarah Mozengo - Consent of
    Sarah Mozengo dated 17 May 1802 - Bond not filled in -
    Name of surety gone.

Fergusson, James T. & Fanny Davis 8 Jan. 1823, William Brickey,
    Jr. sec.

Gallagher, Augustus L. & Fanney Elmore 9 Jan. 1817, Joseph
    Elmore sec.
Gallagher, Peter & Betsy Garner - Consent of Betsy Garner dated
    27 Oct. 1800
Gallagher, Peter B. & Lydia E. B. Garner 15 June, 1837, William
    Beale sec.

Garnett, Henry T. & Eliza L. Waring 12 Oct. 1822, Robert G.
    Robb sec.

Garland, Benjamin N. & Sarah McClannahan 3 Dec. 1833, John H.
    McClannahan sec.

Garner, Alexander & (blank) 24 Mar. 1800, Thomas Johnston sec.
Garner, Daniel & Nancy Brann 28 Jan. 1806, Matthew Brann sec.
Garner, Dozier & Mary Beale 2 Jan. 1821, John Beale sec.
Garner, Dosiah & Frances Wroe, dau. Mary Wroe 23 Feb. 1828,
    Samuel C. Wroe sec.
Garner, George & Anne Middleton 31 Mar. 1790, Vincent Garner sec.
Garner, Gerrard & Nancy Hull 13 July 1787, William Coward sec.
Garner, Griffin G. & Mary Griggs 14 Dec. 1798, Henry Griggs sec.
Garner, James G. & Elizabeth W. Hudson 25 Nov. 1835, John M.
    Burke sec.
Garner, Jeremiah & Deborah Moss 5 Nov. 1793
Garner, John & Nancy Angel 12 Oct. 1796, Edmund R. Jeffries sec.
Garner, John & Elizabeth Brewer 8 June 1821, Elija Spurling sec.
Garner, Presley & Caty Askins 17 Dec. 1805, Thomas Williams sec.
Garner, Samuel & Sarah Billings 20 Mar. 1805, Reubin Spurling sec.
Garner, Spencer & Alice Bailey Washington 6 Mar. 1798, George
    Washington sec.
Garner, Thomas A. & Margaret P. Johnson 28 Apr. 1828, William
    Holliday sec.
Garner, Vincent M. & Margaret L. Dement 13 May 1848, Peter L.
    Self sec.
Garner, Willis & Magdaline Crabb, sister of Daniel Crabb, consent
    of Daniel Crabb dated 20 Dec. 1803 & Bond signed but not
    filled in - William Courtney sec.

Garner, Willis & Frances Lamkin 25 Nov. 1805, Samuel Crabb sec.

Gaskins, Bartler & Mary Ann Peck 21 Oct. 1829, Sam'l Harrison sec.
Gaskins, Patrick & Sarah Gaskins 14 Jan. 1842, William Bailey sec.

Gaun, Alexander & Lettice Garner 15 Dec. 1807, William Brann sec.

Gawen, William & Alice Jefferson Garner, dau. Catherine Garner,
    14 Dec. 1818, Augustus L. Gallagheare sec.

Gibbs, Charles & Nancy (W?)illiams -- Nov. 1787, William------
    sec. - Badly damaged.
Gibbs, Charles E. & Elizabeth Miller 26 Dec. 1844, Joseph E.
    Moxley sec.
Gibbs, John & P. C. Askins, 7 Oct. 1817, Charles S. Askins sec.

Gibson, Robert & Margaret Mazarett 23 Nov. 1795, James Triplett
    sec.

Gilbert, William & Elenor Porter, dau. Demcey Porter, 30 Dec.
    1793, William Porter sec.

Glascock, George, Jr. & Mary Jane McCance 29 Dec. 1830, Robert
    Beale, Jr. sec.
Glascock, Syms C. & Elizabeth Middleton 23 Jan. 1797, Thomas
    Plummer sec. - Badly damaged.

Glasby, George W. & Virginia M. Harvey 23 Dec. 1844, Joseph F.
    Harvey sec.

Goldsmith, Dr. John & Julia Arnold alias Lovell, spinster,
    dau. John Lovell, 17 Jan. 1788, John Piper sec.

Good, Barnett & Elizabeth Weaver 14 May 1806, Thomas Weaver sec.
Goode, John & Sally Bettisworth - Consent of William Bettisworth
    dated 10 Apr. 1803 - Bond signed but not filled in -
    Charles Bettisworth sec.

Gordon, Peter & Susan Lee of Leesville, 24 May 1808, Baldwin M.
    Lee sec.

Gouldin, Jesse & Peggy Moxley 19 Aug. 1793, Richard Moxley sec.

Grant, James & Sarah Lambert, wid. 10 Nov. 1794, George Garner sec.

Granshan, John & Elizabeth Butler 26 Dec. 1825, William A. Butler
    sec.

Graham, John & Molley F. Middleton - Consent of Peter P. Cox
    of Federal Hill, guardian of Molley F. Middleton -
    Bond dated 12 Oct. 1801, Thomas Plummer sec.

Green, Charles B. & Olivia A. Spilman 19 Dec. 1848, Bushrod W.
    Spilman sec.

Green, Charles D. & Margaret B. Eliff30 Jan. 1844, Henry Eliff
    sec.
Green, James & Susanna Dunton 16 Dec. 1794, Tarpley Short sec.
Green, James & Elizabeth Wilkins 7 Feb. 1833, William Deatley sec.
Green, Jesse & Lucetty Green, dau. Sarah Green, 16 May 1798,
    Charles Green sec.
Green, Nathaniel & Elizabeth Jett, 12 Feb. 1821, Benjamin Simms
    sec.
Green, Nathaniel & Lucy Edmonds 18 May 1829, William Pomroy sec.
Green, Samuel & Elizabeth Edwards 28 Apr. 1789, John Higdon sec.
Green, Whiting & Susannah Ryls -- May 1816, Silas Short sec.

Greenlaw, William & Sally R. Peirce, dau. Joseph Peirce, 13 Apr.
    1796, Ransdell Peirce sec.

Greer, W. J. W. & Louisa Jane Owens 23 Dec. 1848, John Reed sec.

Gregory, George & Ann Fitzgerald 25 Aug. 1792, Thomas Gregory sec.
Gregory, George & Molley Billings 2 Feb. 1811, Thomas Gregory sec.
Gregory, Henry & Nancy Barnet 3 Aug. 1814, Thomas Gregory sec.
Gregory,Henry C. Elizabeth Maskiel 23 Feb. 1839, John B. Carroll
    sec.
Gregory, James & Isabella Templeman 5 Mar. 1812, Gerrard
    McKenney sec.
Gregory, James & Sarah Ann Brown 6 Apr. 1843, John P. Laycock
    sec.
Gregory, John & Nancy Williams 11 July 1797, Thomas Gregory sec.
Gregory, John & Elizabeth Carrel 6 Mar 1810, John Hammon sec.
Gregory, John & Fanny Howson 8 Nov. 1830, Robert Anton sec.
Gregory, John & Maria Ann Kirk 5 Mar. 1838, Griffin Kirk sec.
Gregory, Joseph & Calvert S. Williams 26 Apr. 1819, William
    Courtney sec.
Gregory, Thomas & Elizabeth Cavender 10 Jan. 1807, Robert
    Anderson sec.
Gregory, Thomas & Elizabeth King 29 May 1823, John Gregory sec.
Gregory, Vincent & Elizabeth Garner 29 Dec. 1828, William
    Garner sec.

Griffith, Edward C. & Mary E. Cox 5 Nov. 1838, Joseph Jones sec.

Griggs, Harry & Barbara Lucas 26 Jan. 1814, Campbell Teet sec.
Griggs, Henry & Lucy Dozier 25 Sept. 1820, James Dozier sec.
Griggs, Henry & Sary E. Mothershead 1 Dec. 1849, G. G. Mothers-
    head sec.
Griggs, William & Hannah Self 7 Mar. 1791, Mathew Partridge sec.

Grigsby, Robert & Margaret Deane 5 Apr. 1845, Robert Jackson
    sec.

Grimes, Jonathan & Hannah Mann 17 Feb. 1797, Anthony A. Harrison
    sec.

Grinnan, John & Jane Clarke, dau. Jane Wigley, 15 Jan. 1795
    Sturman Sanford sec.

Grissit, Independent & Frances Washington 22 May 1837, James
　　Yardley
Grissit, James & Jane Winkfield 30 Nov. 1824, Walker Winkfield
　　sec.
Grissit, John & Ann Pursley dau. Mary Wills, 22 July 1793,
　　Ashton Combs sec.
Grissett, Thomas & Mary Murry 12 Jan 1825, John Mozingo sec.
Grisset, William & Sally Pursley 7 Feb. 1837, Henry Winkfield
　　sec.
Grissett, Walker & Martha Deen 11 Dec. 1848, Henry Winkfield
　　sec.

Gutridge, Albert M., son of Elizabeth Gutridge, & Mary Ann Nash
　　1 Feb. 1838, Samuel Roe sec.
Gutridge, Henry & Sally Sneed Morton 28 Oct. 1790, John Morton
　　sec.
Gutridge, Henry R. & Ann White 1 Apr. 1825, Joshua Reamy sec.
Gutridge, Henry & Harriett Pitts, dau. Martha Pitts, 20 Dec
　　1849, William Gutridge sec.
Gutridge, James & Elizabeth Morton 7 Aug. 1798, Jacob Millar sec.
Gutridge, James & Nancy Spillman 25 Jan. 1812, Thomas Gutridge
　　sec.
Gutridge, James & Susan Hinson 11 Jan. 1820, George H. Sisson sec.
Guttridge, James S. & Baynton B. Reamy 16 Dec. 1841, Sam'l Nash
　　sec.
Gutridge, John & Elizabeth Crask 8 May 1804, William Nash sec.
Gutridge, John & Elizabeth Ann Atkins 19 Oct. 1844, Joseph
　　Atkins sec.
Gutridge, Ransdell S. & Mary M. Deatley 22 Jan. 1844, R. D.
　　Deatley sec.
Gutridge, Reubin & Elizabeth Carter 13 July 1797, John Carter
　　sec.
Gutridge, Richard C. & Eliza Reamy, dau. Joshua Reamy, 15 Oct.
　　1832, John Morris, Sr. sec.
Guttridge, Robert & Susan Drake 26 Dec. 1831, Robert Sanders sec.
Guttridge, Thomas & Elizabeth Jenkins 12 Mar. 1837, James
　　Jenkins, Jr. sec.
Gutridge, Warner & Ann Gutridge, dau. James Gutridge, 18 Jan.
　　1848, Henry R. Gutridge sec.
Guttridge, William C. & Lucy Carpenter 16 Dec. 1822, Daniel
　　Carter sec.

Habron, William & Sally Pillien 6 Oct. 1808, William Brann sec.

Hackney, James & Caty Muse 29 Nov. 1797, James Bland sec.
Hackney, Meredith M. & Elizabeth L. Rust, dau. Elizabeth Rust,
　　28 Jan. 1803, W. Sisson sec.

Haislip, Joseph & Sarah A. Hall 13 Dec. 1847, Charles C. Baker
　　sec.

Hail, George & Fanny Cavender -- Mar. 1807, Walter Self sec.

Hails, Newton & Sarah Rose 24 June 1797, Thomas Hails sec.

Hallbrook, Mordeca & Sarah Marmaduke 12 Aug. 1799, Thomas Blundell
    sec.

Hall, Edward & Betsey McGuy 23 July 1791, William L. Hutchings sec.
Hall, Elkridge & Sebina Jenkins 11 Apr. 1787, Smith Jenkins sec.
Hall, Henry & Elizabeth Silba 13 Jan 1837, John Spillman sec.
Hall, Reuben & Winney Knask 19 Dec. 1815, William Hall sec.
Hall, Richard Madison, son of William B. Hall & Henrietta A.
    Healy, dau. Mary A. Healy, 20 May 1846, John Robinson sec.
Hall, Robert & Sabella Rempleman, dau. Samuel Templeman, 19 Jan.
    1825, Stephen D. Pitts sec.
Hall, Robert & Catherine Drake, dau. Ann Pope, 2 Mar. 1842,
    Henry W. Pope sec.
Hall, Rodham, of Northumberland County & Magdalen McClanahan -
    Consent of M. McClanahan dated 12 Sept. 1803, witnessed by
    Jemima S. McClanahan - Bond signed but not filled in -
    Richard McClanahan sec.
Hall, Trusel & Hannah Middleton 13 Jan. 1808, Vincent T. Branson
    sec.
Hall, Trusel B. & Isabell Sandy 21 Mar. 1816, Vincent T. Branson
    sec.
Hall, Trusel B. & Sally Spurling 11 May 1821, Newyear C. Branson
    sec.
Hall, William Williamson & Rachel Sanford 14 Dec. 1844, Edwin G.
    Reed sec.
Hall, William & Molly Olive 30 July 1804, -inge Hall sec.
Hall, William & Betsy Shadrack 6 Jan. 1808, John Baldison sec.
Hall, William & Caty Bruce 4 Apr. 1808, Thomas Crookham sec.
Hall, William & Sally Coats 2 Sept. 1816, William Jinkins sec.
Hall, William B. & Mary Ann Omohundro, dau. Richard Omohundro,
    10 Oct. 1825, George G. Mothershead sec.
Hall, William B. & Mary B. Omohundro 10 Oct. 1843, E. B.
    Omohundro sec.
Hall, William S. & Ann Silba 1 Dec. 1835, Robert C. Tate sec.
Hall, William S. & Mary Pursley 20 Apr. 1837, James Sanders sec.

Hammond, Berry & Polly Grisset, wid. 3 Jan. 1838, Henry Winkfield
    sec.
Hammond, Berry & Kesiah Lucas 26 Sept. 1839, O. E. P. Hazard sec.
Hammond, William E. & Susanna Winkfield 24 May 1838, Henderson
    Marks sec.

Hammons, Newman & Nancy Green 14 June 1813, Joseph Bartlett sec.

Hammock, Benjamin & Patty Scutt, dau. Charles Scutt, 31 Jan. 1792
    Charles Scutt sec.
Hammock, Rodham & Catherine M. Yeatman, dau. Ann H. Yeatman,
    8 Dec. 1838, G. G. Mothershead sec.
Hammock, William & Betsy Pursley, dau. Mary Pursley, 13 Nov.
    1797, Henry Asbury sec.

Hart, James & Peggy Muse 27 Dec. 1791, Richard Muse sec.

Hart, Reubin & Elizabeth Thomas - Not dated - Bond signed but not
filled in. Thomas Spence, Jr. sec.

Harris, Andrew & Anne Hall 30 July 1792, Richard Lowe sec.
Harris, Charles W. & Mary Muse Reed, dau. Joseph B. Reed, 11
June 1844, William R. Sutton sec.
Harris, James & Elizabeth Brown 22 Aug. 1817, William Mothershead
sec.
Harris, Morning & Ann Jarvis Edmonds 26 Jan. 1825, Vincent Edmonds
sec.
Harris, Stephen J. & Eliza J. Weaver 4 Jan. 1844, James Sanders sec.

Harrison, Alexander & Alice Nelson 25 June 1793, Francis W. Smith
sec.
Harrison, Anthony A. & Hannah Sanford 16 July 1795, William
Sanford sec.
Harrison, Daniel C. & Mary Harrison 29 Dec. 1830, Daniel Hardwick
& Thomas Self sec.
Harrison, James & Elizabeth J. Courtney 28 Jan. 1833, Mathew R.
King sec.
Harrison, John & Isabel Jones, vid. 7 Oct. 1786, Edmond Bulger sec.
Harrison, John, son of Samuel Harrison, & Julia Leecock, consent
of Julia Leecock & Samuel Harrison dated 29 Mar. 1817,
witnessed by Jeremiah Leecock.
Harrison, Newman & Agatha Lucas 15 Apr. 1791
Harrison, Samuel & Patty S. Harper 20 May 1790, John Harper sec.
Harrison, Samuel & Letty Henry 19 May 1829, Henry Johnson sec.

Hardwick, Daniel H. & Lucy Smith, dau. Peter Smith, 8 July 1823
George Delano sec.
Hardwick, Daniel & Susan B. Self, dau. Moses Self, 15 Jan. 1834
John Lusby sec.
Hardwick, John & Mary M. Mothershead, dau. G. G. Mothershead, 5
Dec. 1833, James Crask sec.

Hardage, Aaron & Sally Harrison 11 July 1787, Medkitt Gill sec.

Harvey, George C. & Mary Susan Cox, dau. James L. Cox, 18 Dec.
1835, John F. Jett sec.
Harvey, James & Lucette Fox 18 Mar. 1793, Samuel Baker sec.
Harvey, Joseph F. & Ann W. Hungerford 18 Oct. 1843, William Hutt
sec.
Harvey, Octavius & Susanna Maria Muse, dau. Charles Muse, 23
Dec. 1816, Joseph Fox sec.

Harper, William & Polly Self 8 Feb. 1809, Thomas Douglass sec.

Hawkins, James & Mary Reynolds 19 July 1793, William Reynolds sec.
Hawkins, Jonathan & Elender Sullivant 17 Jan. 1805, Charles P.
Hawkins sec.
Hawkins, William & Martha O'Harrow, dau. Thomas O'Harrow, 9 Nov.
1830, Joseph Yeatman sec.

Hawkins, William & Polly King 24 July 1833, Joseph D. Self sec.

Haynie, Prestley & Jane Eliza Butler, dau. James & Elizabeth
    Butler, 22 July 1833, William Ticer sec.
Haynie, Prestly & Sally M. Butler 23 Mar. 1842, William Ticer sec.

Hazzard, Charles & Ann Rice Ringmaden 4 June 1811, Vincent
    Edmonds sec.
Hazard, E. O. P. & Agnes R. Harrison 2 Dec. 1839, William
    Johnson sec.
Hazard, John & Ann Spurling 20 Dec 1827, William Spurling sec.
Hazard, Josiah & Fanny Lewis Ramey 22 Mar. 1803, Joshua Ramey sec.
Hazard, Robert R. & Elizabeth Yeatman, dau. John H. Yeatman, 18
    Mar. 1841, O. E. P. Hazard sec.
Hazard, William & Mary Shadrick 28 Dec. 1791, William Yates sec.
Hazard, William, Jr. & Ann Blundell, wid. 7 Dec. 1796, John
    Grinnan sec.
Hazard, William, Jr. & Mary Ann Barnes, dau. Hannah M. Barnes,
    15 Apr. 1826, Austin Dozier sec.

Head, Benjamin R. & Ann Jett 10 Dec. 1823, Campbell Tete sec.
Head, John S. & Mary Anidd 9 Dec. 1816, Alexander Weaver sec.
Head, Uriah & Mahala Ann Dameron 22 July 1830, William Butler sec.

Headley, William & Louisa Middleton 27 Nov. 1815, Vincent T.
    Branson sec.

Healy, Samuel L. S. & Elizabeth A. Redman 13 Nov. 1847, R. M.
    Hall sec.

Henry, George & Ellen Jackson 18 Oct. 1815, William Henry sec.
Henry, George & Barbary Smith 18 Jan. 1832, Henry Johnson sec.
Henry, William & Sarah Ann Asting 25 Nov. 1846, Henry S.
    Johnson sec.

Hennage, John & Delia James 29 Mar. 1791, John Wood sec.
Henage, William & Ann N. Hazard 20 Mar. 1821, Josiah Hazard sec.

Herndon, R. W. & Margaret G. Peirce 6 Mar. 1836, Graham C. Peirce
    sec.

Hill, George & Rosannah Bunnon 6 Mar. 1788, Nath'l Favours sec.
Hill, Thomas & Martha Peirce 7 June 1787, James Lynch sec.

Hilton, William & Hannah Christopher Stott 13 Feb. 1798, Thomas
    Lyne sec.

Hinson, Austin & Mahaley Hueson 17 Mar. 1829, James Guttridge
    sec.
Hinson, Charles S. & Mary Susan Sampson, dau. Thomas Sampson
    26 Sept. 1842, George M. Carter sec.
Hinson, Fenner & Rebeckah Carpenter 21 July 1824, Beriman Ramey
    sec.

Hinson, George & Elizabeth Tate 20 Sept. 1815, James Deakins sec.

Hinson, James & Nanny Marks 31 July 1798, John Marks sec.

Hinson, James & Sibella Washington, dau. William & Betty
    Washington, 16 May 1807, Richard T. Brown sec.

Hinson, James & Susannah Sanford 1 June 1815, Reuben Sanford sec.

Hinson, Jennings & Fanny Weadon, dau. Sarah Weadon, 25 June 1803
    Daniel Wilson sec.

Hinson, John & Molly Deane 25 Jan. 1791, Campbell Taite sec.

Hinson, John & Sally Sylvia 7 Feb. 1833, William Carter sec.

Hinson, John & Ann Tallant 24 May 1842, Nathaniel H. Beddoe sec.

Hinson, John R. & Susan Hinson 22 Feb. 1845, Meredith Hinson sec.

Hinson, Jonas & Polly Kelley, dau. Molly Kelley, 30 July 1810,
    William Hinson sec.

Hinson, Meriday & Hannah Worsencraft 27 Sept. 1819, James
    Anthoney sec.

Hinson, Meredith & Hannah Whoosencroft 8 Apr. 1820, Ebenezer
    Balderson sec.

Hinson, Meredith & Nelly Coates 7 May 1839, Mortimore Jett sec.

Hinsen, Presley & Caty Peed, dau. Phillip Peed - Not dated -
    Bundle marked "1801" - Consent of Phillip Peed - Bond
    signed but not filled in - John Peed sec.

Hinson, Presley & Ann Hinson 15 Jan. 1849, Meredith Hinson sec.

Hinson, Reubin & Mary M. Hinson, dau. William Hinson, 25 Sept.
    1833, Oliver E. P. Hazard sec.

Hinson, Salathiel L. & Elizabeth Curtis 24 Dec. 1833, Joel L.
    Rose sec.

Hinson, Thomas & Ann Riley 22 Sept. 1841, Rodney Moxley sec.

Hinson, Thornton & Bethiah Sandford 25 July 1816, James Hinson
    sec.

Hinson, Vincent & Fanny Roe 11 Feb. 1829, Thomas P.W.Neale sec.

Hinson, William F. & Mary Ann Neale, dau. Lucinda Miller, 23 Jan.
    1825, Thomas Neale sec.

Hinson, William & Mary E. Burn 16 Aug. 1838, Henry V. Sanders sec.

Hinson, William F. & Elizabeth S. Bryant, dau. Sarah Bryant, 3
    Aug. 1847, Tranville White sec.

Hipkins, Robert Spotwood & Mary Hays Butler, dau. Beckwith Butler,
    1 Nov. 1796, Daniel McCarty sec. (consent of Beckwith
    Butler dated 31 Oct. 1796)

Hipkins, William Aug. & Margaret Martin, dau. Capt. Jacob Martin,
    10 June 1799, Joseph Fox, Jr. sec.

Hodge, Thomas & Caty Washington 15 May 1790, Henry Washington sec.

Hogan, Richard J. & Mary King 10 May 1832, John L. Middleton sec.

Holt, John & Jane Bolderson 26 Jan. 1787, Gilbert Bolderson sec.

Holliday, William & Susan R. Robinson 11 Dec. 1837, Steptoe T.
    Rice sec.

Hollingshead, John & Ellenor Steel 27 June 1808, Christopher
    Deatley sec.

Hooke, James & Susan Jenkins 11 July 1831, James Eidson sec.

Hopkins, Gerrard & Elizabeth S. Theeds, dau. in law of Charles
    Bettisworth, 12 Mar. 1800.

Hore, James & Frances Nelson 9 June 1790, William Brown sec.

Howe, Abner & Nancy Harrison, dau. William Harrison, 30 Nov. 1790
    William Franks sec.

Howell, John & Sally Gregory 24 Jan. 1789, Thomas Gregory sec.
Howell, Thomas & Polly Gregory 3 Dec. 1828, John Anton sec.

Howson, John W. & Martha T. Donnahaue 12 Dec. 1826, John Anton
    sec.
Howson, Sidnor & Elizabeth Sullivan, 27 Feb. 1829, Owen Sullivan
    sec.
Howsen, Stewart & Ann Gregory 27 Apr. 1836, Robert Anton sec.
Howsen, William & Betsy McKenney 1 Sept. 1804, Youell Howson sec.
Howsen, Youell F. & Alesy Howel 21 Mar. 1801, - Consent of Alesy
    Howel dated 21 Mar. 1801.

Hudson, Corbin & Elizabeth Wroe 1 June 1825, Mathew R. King sec.
Hudson, George V. & Lettice Carter 25 Apr. 1814, Griffin Jeffries
    sec.
Hudson, Joseph W. & Mary Ann Pridham 24 Apr. 1843, John English
    sec.
Hudson, Robert & Martha King ------- 1801, Levi Hillard sec.
Hudson, Rodham & Molley Dolman 11 Sept. 1798, John Dolman sec.

Hudnall, John, of Northumberland County, son of Thomas Hudnall
    & Elizabeth Jett 13 Feb. 1787, Anthony Payton sec.
    Badly damaged

Hughs, John & Winefret Hawood 20 Aug. 1791, William Walker sec.

Hull, Gerrard & Ann Robinson 16 Jan. 1787, Edward Porter sec.

Hunter, John & Susan Edwards - Consent of Frances Edwards &
    Richard L. Banten, guardian - Bond signed but not filled
    in.
Hunter, Samuel & Nancy Muse 23 Dec. 1801, John Hunter sec.
Hunter, Thomas & Maria S. Tennent, dau. Anna S. Tennent, 4 Dec.
    1832, H. M. Tennent sec.
Hunter, William & Fanny Marmaduke 26 Nov. 1793, John Hunter sec.
Hunter, Thomas H., of Northumberland County, & Sarah Jane
    Sandford, 21 Mar. 1836, James Hurst & Thomas H. Pinchard
    sec.

Hungerford, Henry & Amelia Spence 12 Mar. 1818, Thomas Spence
    Sr. sec.
Hungerford, Maj. Henry & Mary A. Spence 11 Sept. 1834, William
    G. Sturman sec.
Hungerford, John W. & Sophia Muse, dau. Walker Muse, 19 Nov. 1810
    Richard T. Brown sec.

Hutt, Edwin, son of Gerard Hutt, & Nancy N.McClannahan,dau. John
McClannaham, 29 Nov. 1837, O. E. P. Hazard sec.
Hutt, Gerard, Sr. & Elizabeth Batten 1 Oct. 1832, William Young
Sturman sec.
Hutt, Hiram & Ann P. Marmaduke, dau. Vincent Marmaduke, 25 Feb.
1833, Dempsey Porter sec.
Hutt, Solomon & Molly P. Redman 18 Dec. 1818, Thomas S.Rice sec.
Hutt, Steptoe D. & Eliza A. Hazard 27 Jan. 1845, O.E.P.Hazard sec.
Hutt, Thomas & Mary Sturman 4 Sept. 1792, William Spark sec.
Hutt, Thomas W. & Ann Omohundro 24 July 1827, William Y. Sturman
sec.
Hutt, William Spence & Constance U. E. Villard 18 June, 1794,
Andrew Joseph Villard sec.
Hutt, William & Elizabeth J. Harvey 10 Jan. 1828, Joseph S.
Lyell sec.

Hutchings, William Sutton, son of John Hutchings, & Nancy
Cavender, dau. Thomas Cavender, 22 Apr. 1791, James Sorrell
sec.
Hutchings, William & Franky Curtis 3 June 1799, Vincent Branson
sec.

Ingram, Orron & Sally A. Redman 26 Jan. 1829, Solomon Hutt sec.

Inscoe, Edward & Jane Winkfield 15 July 1820, John Burges sec.
Inscoe, Thomas & Frances Bailey, dau. Michael Bailey, 24 Jan.
1811, William Rogers sec.

Insley, Abel & Polly Parks, dau. Arthur Parks, 19 May 1825,
Robert Bailey sec.

Jacobs, Henry L. & Peggy Garner, dau. Samuel Garner - Consent
of Samuel Garner dated 15 Jan. 1803 - Bond signed but
not filled in - Thomas Clusky sec.

Jackson, Bernard & Sally Claxton, dau. Jeremiah Claxton, 29
June 1793, Thomas Claxton sec.
Jackson, Christopher & Rockey Holland 20 Feb. 1793, William
Atwell sec.
Jackson, George, of Richmond County, & Naney J. Cole - Consent of
Peggy Cole dated 1 Apr. 1822, witnessed by Samuel J.
Booth - Bond signed but not filled in - Samuel J. Booth sec.
Jackson, Henry & Harriot Stuart, dau. in law of George Fitzhugh -
Consent of George Fitzhugh dated "Twiford, 17 Oct. 1800"
witnessed by Samuel Jackson & Sophia Bland - Bond signed
but not filled in - Samuel Jackson sec.
Jackson, Newman B. & Mary Garner 28 Dec. 1815, William Bulger
sec.
Jackson, Richard & Sophia Scales, dau. James Scales, 13 Mar. 1821,
M. C. Harvey sec.
Jackson, Richard L. & Lucinda Deatly 24 Nov. 1828, James Deatley
sec.

Jackson, Thomas & Polly Brown - Consent of Polly Brown dated 23
Sept. 1809, witnessed by James Weaver - Bond signed but
not filled in - James Weaver sec.
Jackson, William & Martha Oldham 21 May 1822, Benedict Walker sec.

James, Abner & Lucinda Payton 10 Aug. 1821, Vincent Barrock sec.
James, Sherrod & Fanney Deatley 30 Nov. 1809 -------------------
Badly damaged.
James, Thomas & Ann Goldman 23 Mar. 1846, Ransdell S. Gutridge sec.

Jeffries, Enock G. & Ann Murphy, dau. Murdock Murphy, 7 Mar. 1831
Robert H. Chowning sec.
Jeffries, Enock G. & Elizabeth C. Wright, dau. Hannah Wright, 28
July 1834, Robert Bailey sec.
Jeffries, Jeremiah, Jr. & Jane Jeffries ---- 1804, Jeremiah
Jeffries sec.
Jeffries, Jeremiah & Mary Ingham 3 Aug. 1841, Joseph F.Harvey sec.
Jeffries, Robert W. & Ann S. Robinson, dau. Hannah Robinson, 17
Dec. 1833, Joseph Robinson sec.

Jenkins, Benjamin & Susanna Pullin 14 Jan. 1817, James Hinson sec.
Jenkins, Davis & Sarah Selvey 19 Dec. 1809, Abraham Selvey sec.
Jenkins, Harmon & Catherine Carter -- 1801, John Morton sec.
Jenkins, James & Peggy Guttridge 15 Jan. 1810, Robert Jenkins sec.
Jenkins, James & Frances Bartlett 1 Jan. 1817, John Sanders sec.
Jenkins, James P. & Ann Moxley 27 Oct. 1831, Jacob V.Doleman sec.
Jenkins, John & Elizabeth Mothershead 27 Oct. 1890, William
Sanford sec.
Jenkins, John B. & Martha Omohundro 22 Feb. 1796, Smith Jenkins
sec.
Jenkins, John B. & Winifred L. Payne 31 Dec. 1804, Thomas
Omohundro sec.
Jenkins, John S. & Harriett H. Hunter 4 June 1845, M. M. Marma-
duke, Jr. sec.
Jenkins, Joseph L. & Frances Bulger 2 Nov. 1842, George H. Sisson
sec.
Jenkins, Matthew & Elizabeth D. Eidson, dau. John Eidson, Sr.
12 Jan. 1819, John Eidson, Sr. sec.
Jenkins, Reuben & Rachel Sanders 3 July 1815, John Bowing sec.
Jenkins, Reubin & Margaret Barker, dau. Elizabeth Jett, 2 Sept.
1839, John Barker sec.
Jenkins, Reuben & Ann Rawlet 29 Dec. 1842, Matthew Wilkins sec.
Jenkins, Richard W. &. Catharine Barrott 29 Dec. 1832, William
Omohundro sec.
Jenkins, Robert & Nancy Kelly 26 Feb. 1810, William Oliff sec.
Jenkins, Smith & Jemima Washington - Agreement dated 6 Dec. 1792
Witnessed by Thomas Washington, Ann Washington &
William Omohundro
Jenkins, Thomas & Sarah Green 28 Mar. 1808, Sam'l Mothershead sec.
Jenkins, Thomas M. & Ann P. Hunter 22 Jan. 1821, Charles Mothers-
head sec.
Jenkins, Thomas B. & Elizabeth Dozier 3 Mar. 1835, Henry Griggs
sec.
Jenkins, Thomas B. & Mahaley A. Reamey 9 Mar. 1846, Thomas
Sanford sec.

Jenkins, William & Felicia Hinson 16 Mar. 1831, James Johnson sec.
Jenkins, William & Felicia King 25 Dec. 1845, William S. Cullerson
    sec.
Jenkins, William & Sarah Thompson, dau. James Thompson, 3 Jan.
    1849, Solomon Dixon sec.
Jenkins, William H. & Lucy Yeatman 18 May 1831, James Mariner sec.

Jessee, William J. & Mary D. M. Tapscott, dau. John G. Tapscott,
    28 June 1830, John G. Tapscott sec.

Jett, Charles C. & Mary W. B. Towles 30 May 1825, Henry D. Stocke
    sec.
Jett, Cyrus & Jane Settle dau. Ann Settle, 2 Oct. 1841, A. S.
    King sec.
Jett, Francis & Sally Sims 19 Dec. 1793, William Jett sec.
Jett, James & Nancy Muse, dau. Thomas Muse, 25 Feb. 1805, Dan'l
    Carmichael sec.
Jett, James H. & Jane White 23 Mar. 1831, William White sec.
Jett, John & Frances James 10 Mar. 1789, John Drake sec.
Jett, Steohen & Elizabeth D. Muse, dau. Thomas Muse, 13 May 1805
    John Jett sec.
Jett, Thornton & Margaret Cullison 7 Jan. 1826, James Johnson sec.
Jett, Thomas & Peggy Berkley 26 Nov. 1793, Samuel Berrymau sec.
Jett, William, Jr. & Pheby Short, dau. Patsy Short, 3 Mar. 1806
    William Jett Sr. sec.
Jett, William & Catharine White 25 Nov. 1807, Vincent Barreck
    sec.
Jett, William & Nancy Thomas 14 Dec. 1809, Reuben Hart sec.
Jett, William J. & Lucinda James 9 Apr. 1827, Thomas James sec.
Jett, William J. & Mary Simms -- Nov. 1828, Thomas H. Micom sec.

Jewell, James & Moley Martin Ringmaiden 19 Dec. 1792, John
    Redman sec.
Jewell, James, of Richmond County, & Haney Brewer - Consent of
    Haney Brewer dated 13 May 1808, Witnessed by James
    Brewer - Bond signed but not filled in - Daniel Marma-
    duke sec.
Jewell, James & Elizabeth Burn 22 May 1826, Robert Hall scc.
Jewell, William & Mary Carroll 1 Dec. 1809, James Jewell sec.

Jewett, John & Barbary McKenney 10 July 1805, George Nash sec.

Jinkins, John & Rebecca Brown 31 Oct. 1808, John Bowing sec.
Jinkins, Robert & Betsy B. Mitchell 5 Mar. 1813, Thomas Jinkins
    sec.
Jinkins, Thomas & Mary Hill 10 Aug. 1813, James Carpenter sec.

Johnson, Benjamin & Peggy Sandford 29 Jan. 1822, Josiah Hazard
    sec.
Johnson, Benjamin & Sarah Jenkins 14 Oct. 1844, John Beddoo sec.
Johnson, Benedict & Fanny Lyell,-Jan. 1827, John M. Bronson sec.
Johnson, George & Muriel V. Dye 26 July 1815, Thomas Johnson sec.
Johnson, Isaack & Betsey Hinson 2 June 1801, George Field sec.
Johnson, Jacob & Betsy Nelson 29 Sept. 1790, John Brown, Jr. sec.

Johnson, James & Elizabeth Morriss 23 Mar. 1801, Thomas Gregory
    sec.

Johnson, James & Mary Branson 4 Feb. 1809, William Butler sec.

Johnson, James K. & Harriot W. Redman 1 Feb. 1826, William G.
    Morris sec.

Johnson, James & Ann Franklin 21 Dec. 1835, Thomas Franklin sec.

Johnson, James & Mary Franklin 23 Jan. 1839, Thomas Franklin sec.

Johnson, James & Susan Thompson, dau. Bennett Thompson, 28 Dec.
    1842, Henry Johnson sec.

Johnson, John Green & Nancy Bettisworth, dau. John Bettisworth,
    2 Mar. 1791, James Green sec.

Johnson, John & Harry Tate 25 Dec. 1809, Edmond Tate sec.

Johnson, Johnson & Fanny McKenny 17 Feb. 1846, Daniel Maiden sec.

Johnson, Joseph & Sarah Potter 6 Mar. 1848, Robert McKildoe sec.

Johnson, Josiah & Leanah Head 20 Feb. 1827, Uriah E. Head sec.

Johnson, Osmond & Ann H. Crask 16 Feb. 1821, Charles Mothershead
    sec.

Johnson, Reuben & Fanny Johnson 21 Jan. 1829 Sam'l Johnson sec.

Johnson, Richard B. & Lucetta Massey 30 Aug. 1799, Thomas Massey
    sec.

Johnson, Samuel & Elizabeth Cannaday 15 May 1790, James Taite sec.

Johnson, Samuel & Sarah Hinson, dau. William Hinson, 23 Nov. 1793
    John Hinson sec.

Johnson, Samuel & Juda Johnson 14 Nov. 1827, Alexander Thompson
    sec.

Johnson, Spencer & Hannah Williams 15 Feb. 1787, Alexander Gawin
    sec.

Johnson, Thomas & Ellen Hopkins 31 Dec. 1816, Elisha Spurling sec.

Johnson, Thomas & Rebecca Anton 10 Oct. 1825, George R. Pitts sec.

Johnson, Thomas & Hannah Hubbard 30 July 1830, Edmund Tate sec.

Johnson, William & Molly Redman 21 Dec. 1813, Robert Long sec.

Johnson, William & Peggy Smith 11 Mar. 1818, Thomas L. Rice sec.

Johnson, William & Elizabeth A. Mothershead 12 Dec. 1822, Daniel
    Mothershead sec.

Johnson, William & Ethelenda Rose 1 Oct. 1827, William J. Jett sec.

Johnston, George A. W. & Ann F. Johnston 24 Dec. 1807, William
    Johnston sec.

Johnston, James & Elizabeth Davis 27 May 1807, James Deane sec.

Johnston, William & Ann Deane - Consent of Ann Deane dated 10
    Feb. 1807 - Bond signed but not filled in - George
    Johnston sec.

Jones, Benjamin F. & Alice J. Monroe 8 Oct. 1831, Richard Monroe
    sec.

Jones, Griffin & Sarah Boyd 15 June 1787, David Taylor sec.

Jones, Hiram & Jane Edmonds, dau. Richard Edmonds, 31 Jan. 1850
    Robert A. Jenkins sec.

Jones, James & Sarah Pope, dau. Peneliper Pope, 26 Dec. 1821,
    Joseph Fox sec.

Jones, John & Nancy Burruss, both of the County of Richmond,
    Parish of Lunenburg - Consent of Nancy Burruss dated 22
    Dec. 1800, Witnessed by Samuel Ryals - Bond signed but
    not filled in - Samuel Ryals sec.

Jones, Dr. Joseph & Mary F. Chandler 5 June 1845, William D. Nelson sec.

Jones, Leven & Frances Hall,(21 years old 4 June, 1804), 12 Dec. 1803, Isaac Hall sec.

Jones, Thomas & Polly Tete, 19 Oct. 1824, Thomas Neale sec.

Jones, Thomas & Ann S. Trowbridge 14 Oct. 1843, Joseph F. Harvey sec.

Jones, Travis & Nancy Wright Davis 27 Sept. 1787, George Harrison sec.

Jones, Vincent & Martha Jenkins 30 May 1814, Billy Sanders sec.

Jones, William & Susan Sanders 3 Jan. 1826, Thomas Sanders sec.

Jordan, Cupid & Lucy Adams 4 Jan. 1802, Henry Sisson sec.

Jordan, Reuben & Amelia P. Hall 9 Feb. 1797, John M. Hall sec.

Kelsick, John B. & Elizabeth M. Self 19 Dec. 1831, John C. Beale sec.

Kelton, Ammi & Nancy Fisher 28 Dec. 1815, Henry Maskiel sec.

Kelly, John & Elizabeth Weaver 13 Mar. 1834, Jonathan Bryant sec.

Kelly, Vincent & Attoway Astin, dau. Winneyford Astin, 19 Jan. 1831, Emanuel Smith sec.

Kendall, Jesse & Sukey Sanford 4 Aug. 1813, Joshua Sanford sec.

Kendal, William & Penelope Bartlett 18 Nov. 1816, Thomas Bartlett sec.

Kew, John & Jane Payton 11 Feb. 1787, William Payton sec.

Kew, John & Mary Pursley 9 May 1800, George Field sec.

Kilman, Martin & Frankey Briant 23 Dec. 1819, Levi Briant sec.

Killmon, Martin, Jr. & Fanny Briant, dau. Frances Briant, 11 May 1825, James Briant sec.

Killmon, Martin & Ann Weaver 10 Feb. 1845, Burrell S. Eskridge sec.

King, Griffin & Ann H. English 13 Apr. 1824, Vincent Douglass sec.

King, Henry & Milly Dishman, sister of Sam'l Dishman, 2 July 1833, Samuel Dishman sec.

King, Henry P. & Elizabeth N. Dobbins 22 Feb. 1841, James O. King sec.

King, James & Elender Anderson 7 Nov. 1792, John Bayne sec.

King, James & Mary King, consent of Mary Spurling, 22 Feb. 1819 William Hazard sec.

King, James & Felicia Simms 30 Dec. 1835, George G. Barock sec.

King, Jeremiah & Alcey Stephens, dau. James B. Stephens, 5 Aug. 1825, William Stephens sec.

King, John & Alice Wrow -- 1798, Jeremiah Oldham sec.

King, John & Elizabeth Fisher 26 Feb. 1834, Jeremiah King sec.

King, John R. & Ann C. Brown 27 Apr. 1829, William King sec.

King, John T. & Julyett Mothershead 24 Dec. 1830, Thomas Mothershead sec.

King, John W. & Ann Beale 30 Dec. 1841, James O. King sec.
King, Mathew R., son of Sally King, & Martha Harrison, 1 Feb.
    1825, Rodham Douglas sec.
King, Nathaniel & Elizabeth Briscoe 25 Feb. 1813, William
    Coghill sec.
King, Nathaniel, Jr. & Elizabeth Briscoe 20 Dec. 1817, George
    King sec.
King, Richard R. & Frances Shirley 12 Jan. 1847, William Wroe sec.
King, Smith, Jr. & Jane Middleton Self, dau. Henry Self, 12 Jan.
    1790, Thomas Walker sec.
King, Smith, Sr. & Anne Lamkin 22 Dec. 1801, Robert Hudson sec.
King, William & Ann King, dau. James King, 4 Oct. 1810, James
    King sec.
King, William &Jr. & Sally Robinson 20 Mar. 1816, Griffin King
    sec.
King, William & Mary Pillian (sic) 28 Oct. 1816, Charles C. Rice
    sec.
King, William & Mary Dameron 22 Jan. 1824, James King sec.

Kirk, James & Sarah Simkins 13 Jan. 1819, James Bailey sec.
Kirk, James R. & Margaret E. G. Brown, dau. Fanny Brown, 21 Feb.
    1843, John C. Gregory sec.
Kirk, John & Elender McKenny, wid. 9 Apr. 1790, Thomas Gregory
    sec.
Kirk, John & Nancy Beddus 8 Mar. 1821, Gerard A. Sanford sec.
Kirk, Randall & Elizabeth Brinn 3 Mar. 1792, James King sec.
Kirk, Thomas & Susan Hall 5 May 1825, Williamson Hall sec.
Kirk, Thomas & Sibby Waughan 18 Jan. 1849, William J. Middleton
    sec.
Kirk, William G. & Mary Whealler, sister of Richard Whealler,
    6 Jan. 1824, Griffin R. Kirk

Knox, Elijah & Frances Alverson, dau. Zachariah & Kissiah Alverson,
    7 Sept. 1812, James Nash sec.

Lacy, Joseph & Patsy Hammock Scott, dau. Charles Scott, -- Apr.
    1807, Zachariah Scott sec.
Lacy, Lamkin & Elizabeth Morse 3 Mar. 1801, Ebenezer Morse sec.
Lacy, Theophilus A. & Mary E. Peake, dau. C. Peake, 25 Mar. 1828,
    Jacob R. Richards sec.
Lacey, William & Nancy Davis 27 Apr. 1818, James Davis sec.

Lamb, David & Ann Bryant 21 Jan. 1822, Tarpley Briant sec.

Lamkin, Benedict & Elizabeth B. English 17 May 1825, Benedict
    Walker sec.
Lamkin, Fleet & Charlotte Settle 30 Dec. 1795, William Redman sec.
Lamkin, Fleet & Elender Chilton 27 May 1818, George Brennon sec.
Lamkin, George & Ursley Payne, dau. Ann Payne, 10 Jan. 1822,
    William Redman sec.
Lamkin, Samuel Jr. & Ann Wilkerson 17 Oct. 1827, Robert T. Parker
    sec.

Lamkin, Thomas & Elizabeth B. Morgan 29 Dec. 1823, Mottrom M.
    Wright sec.

Lawrence, James & Winnefer Ross 23 Nov. 1786, Jesse Briger sec.
Lawrence, William & Ursley Sanford 4 July 1808, Spencer Mullins
    sec.

Laycock, Edward _ Polly B. Wilkins 3 Jan. 1823, Hiram King sec.
Laycock, John P. & Phebey Johnson 30 Mar. 1819, William Spurling
    sec.
Laycock, John P. & Ann McKenney 26 Jan. 1824, James McKenney sec.
Laycock, John P. & Elizabeth Brown 29 May 1834, Nelson R. Dozier
    sec.
Laycock, Jeremiah & Elizabeth Kenner 23 Sept. 1794, Daniel Laycock
    sec.

Leblanc, Allen P. & Fanny Hilliard 9 June 1821, W. M. Hilliard sec.

Lee, Henry, Jr. & Ann R. McCarty 24 Mar. 1817, Richard Stuart sec.
Lee, Ludwell & Flora Lee 22 Jan. 1788, Henry Lee sec.
Lee, Thomas, Sr. & Mildred Washington 13 Oct. 1788, William A.
    Lee sec.
Lee, William L. & Sarah McKinney 20 Apr. 1829, James McKinney sec.

Leland, Samuel A. M. & Eliza M. Campbell, dau. Eliza F. Campbell,
    5 Dec. 1836, Will: Newton sec.

Lendrum, Peter & Elizabeth Adkins 16 May 1818, William L. Mothers-
    head sec.

Lefever, John & Eliza A. Carroll 6 Jan. 1849, Joseph H. Moone sec.
Lefever, Nathaniel & Winney Short 3 May 1820, William Short sec.
Lefever, Nathaniel & Martha Pursley 20 Oct. 1838, William Peed
    sec.
Lefever, Nathaniel & Mariah Peed 7 June 1848, George H. Sisson sec.
Lefever, Phineas & Abby Peed dau. Alisay Peed, 8 Mar. 1813,
    James Peed sec.

Lewis, Charles & Ann Head, dau. Rachel Head .- Consent of Ann Head
    dated 20 Nov. 1823, witnessed by Uriah E. Head - Bond
    signed but not filled in - Uriah E. Head sec.
Lewis, Fielding & Catherine D. Lewis, 5 Jan. 1847, John B. Lewis
    sec.
Lewis, Francis & Catherine Smith 22 Dec. 1821, Baldwin M. Lee sec.
Lewis, George & Hannah Thomas 30 Apr. 1793, John Thomas sec.
Lewis, James & Jane Ashton 30 Dec. 1845, Blain Ashton sec.
Lewis, Jeremiah & Elizabeth Moore 30 May 1822, Daniel Harrison sec.
Lewis, John B. & Elizabeth S. Biggs, stepdau. John Stevens, 22
    July, 1844, Thomas L. Garnett sec.
Lewis, Samuel L. & Catherine D. Bowcock, ------------------
    Hannibal Chandler sec.
Lewis, Thomas & Mary Ann Bryant 2 July 1849, Martin Killmon sec.

Linthicum, Francis & Sally Jones, dau. Charles Jones, 29 Mar.
    1826, Daniel Porter sec.

Linthicum, Francis & Martha Omohundro 10 Jan. 1829, G. G.Mothers-
head sec.

Lindsay, Opie & Frankey Jett 21 Dec. 1787, Beckwith Butler sec.

Littrell, William & Keziah Marmaduke 17 July 1801, George Field
sec.

Locust, John & Sarah Kelly 5 Jan. 1791, Thomas Deacons sec.

Long, Charles B. & Sarah F. Sutton, dau. Priscilla Sutton, 17 Feb.
1837, J. W. Sutton sec.

Long, Robert, & Polly Hazzard 28 Feb. 1814, William Hazard sec.

Longworth, George & Molley Landman 24 Feb. 1797, William Longworth sec.

Lorr, James R. & Fanny Gregory, dau. Thomas Gregory, 2 Feb. 1824
George E. Roper sec.

Lucas, Detworth & Margaret Lewis 19 Jan. 1841, Samuel Sutton sec.
Lucas, Elliott & Jane Teet, 14 June 1838, Henry Lucas sec.
Lucas, Henry & Frances Lucas, dau. Meredith Lucas, 12 May 1837,
Henry Winkfield sec.
Lucas, Meredith & Jenny Pope 4 Mar. 1815, Campbell Teet sec.
Lucas, Meredith & Elizabeth Dekins 15 Dec. 1830, Thomas Jones sec.
Lucas, Nathaniel & Nelly Lawrence 31 May 1791, John Lucas sec.
Lucas, Octavius & Robinett Tate 13 July 1843, Henry Tate sec.
Lucas, Samuel & Susanna Silva 27 Dec. 1835, William Pomroy sec.
Lucas, Spencer & Jane Yardley 27 May 1810, James Mothershead sec.
Lucas, Tarpley & Eliza Barker 17 Dec. 1829, James Deakins sec.
Lucas, William N. & Nancy Washington 27 Dec. 1839, William R.
Sisson sec.

Lumkin, Benedict & Molley King 29 Mar. 1789, Smith King sec.

Lusby, John & Margaret Self --Dec. 1833, Daniel Hardwick sec.

Luttrell, Richard & Elizabeth Ellmore 14 Jan. 1795, Thomas
Cluskey sec.
Luttrell, William & Elizabeth Marmaduke 25 Apr. 1795, John Gordon
sec.
Luttrell, William & Lorinda Q. Marmaduke 21 Mar 1835, Charles
Mothershead sec.

Lyell, Dozier & Fanny Smith dau. Peggy Smith, 22 Aug. 1811,
Vincent Dozier sec.
Lyell, John & Sarah Robinson 30 Dec. 1788, Thomas Dozier sec.
Lyell, John & Lucy Sanford, dau. Charles Sanford, 8 Dec. 1796,
John Sanford sec.
Lyell, John A. & Sarah A. J. Plummer 16 Dec. 1822, William Porter
sec.
Lyell, Joseph L. & Susan R. Dishman 25 Mar. 1830, Joseph F. Harvey
sec.

Lyell, Richard M. & Sarah D. Atwell 23 Nov. 1846, William Hutt sec.
Lyell, Samuel & Peggy S. McKildoe 8 Dec. 1807, Richard T. Brown sec.
Lyell, Thomas S. & Mary E. Graham 13 Jan. 1825, William Lyell sec.
Lyell, William H. & Frances Jane Sutton 3 Sept. 1849, W. R. Sutton sec.

Lynch, Patrick & Delily Dodd 11 Dec. 1790, James Dodd sec.

Lyne, Thomas & Susannah Morris, dau. Charles Morris, 28 Nov. 1796, John Butler sec.

McCarty, Daniel & Margaret Robinson, dau. William Robinson, dec., 2 Sept. 1797, James Bland sec.

McCluske, James & Elizabeth Moxley - Consent of Benjamin Bramham, Guardian, dated 27 Nov. 1810, Witnessed by Thomas Stowers Bond signed but not filled in - John McNeil sec.
McClusky, Jerry & Juliann Coward 26 Apr. 1831, William Ga--------

McCoy, George & Nancy McCoy 4 Jan. 1808, William Bran sec.
McCoy, Jarrard & Winney Davis - Consent of Winney Davis dated 17 Mar. 1801
McCoy, Rodham & Elizabeth Brinn 28 Dec. 1816, William King sec.

McCullock, William H. & Mary W. Douglass, dau. James Douglass, 8 Nov. 1816, Benjamin Stuard sec.

McGinney, John & Sally Hedley 27 July 1801, John Watson sec.

McGinnis, Richard & Calista E. Bartlett 14 Dec. 1835, Samuel T. Reamy sec.
McGinniss, Samuel N. & Jane Riley 18 Mar. 1848, James Barrott sec.

McGuire, Alexander & Elizabeth Sutton 14 Feb. 1811, John Brown sec.
McGuire, James & Mary Ann Porter 3 June 1848, Sam'l Sutton sec.
McGuire, John & Mary Pillsbury 3 Feb. 1809, Jeremiah Davis sec.
McGuire, John & Julia Ann Mothershead 10 Mar. 1834, William McGuire sec.
McGuire, John & Sarah M. Bartlett 5 May 1849, G. G. Mothershead sec.
McGuire, Robinson & Mary Hall, dau. Youell Davis, 2 Oct. 1806, Ewell Davis sec.
McGuire, Travis & Beckey Sutton 3 Feb. 1809, Joseph Sutton sec.
McGuire, Vincent & Frances McKenney, wid. 2 Dec. 1806, Newman McKenney sec.
McGuire, William & Lucy Thomas 7 Feb. 1827, Henry Pritchet sec.

McGuy, Bennett & Hannah Eckles 1 Dec. 1787, James McGuy sec.
McGuy, James & Molly Collins 12 Jan. 1790. Smith King sec.
McGuy, Rodam & Mary Askins 23 Dec. 1793, John Kirk sec.

McKildoe, James & Eliza M. Bragg 5 Jan. 1830, Samuel R. Thrift sec.
McKildoe, Robert & Bettey Sanford, wid. 3 June 1796, William R.
Dozier sec.
McKildoe, Robert & Elizabeth Rose, dau. Bennett Rose, 18 Jan. 1837
Benedict Middleton sec.
McKildoe, William & Polly Self, dau. William Self - Consent of
William Self dated 26 Oct. 1803 - Bond signed but not
filled in - Thomas Brown sec.

McKenney, Allen & Alice McKenney 15 Mar. 1815, Newman McKenney sec.
McKenny, Armstrong & Jane Steward 12 Aug. 1813, Nath'l Clapton sec.
McKinney, Baldwin & Jane Sutton 22 Jan. 1844, James McKenny sec.
McKenny, Benjamin & Molley McKenny 22 Mar. 1793, Youell Brinnon
sec.
McKenney, George & Elizabeth McGuire 29 July 1791, William Brown,
Sr. sec.
McKenney, Gerard & Peggy Templeman 7 Dec. 1791, Samuel Templeman
sec.
McKenney, Gerard, Jr. & Frances Sutton, 24 Dec. 1799, Gerard
McKenney sec.
McKenney, Gerard & Peggy Sisson 10 Feb. 1807, William M. Walker
sec.
McKinney, Gerard A. & Elizabeth T. Connellee 23 Dec. 1828,
Reubin McKenney sec.
McKenney, Gerard & Polly Christopher Lewis, dau. Edward D. Lewis,
29 Dec. 1823, Christopher Lewis sec.
McKenney, Gerard R. & Amelia P. Dozier 30 Nov. 1833, John
Hunter sec.
McKenney, James & Sally Sutton 16 Dec. 1806, Daniel Morris sec.
McKenny, John & Peggy Sutton 17 Mar. 1789, Presley McKenny sec.
McKenney, Newman & Alsey McGuire 5 Sept. 1805, William McGuire
sec.
McKenney, Newman & Alice V. McKenney 19 Sept. 1838, Hiram Hutt
sec.
McKenney, Presley, Jr. & Nancy McKenney 31 July 1797, Gerrard
McKenney sec.
McKenney, Richard & Alice B. Potter 7 Jan. 1824, Presley McKenney
sec.
McKenney, Samuel & Priscilla R. Sutton 5 Jan. 1847, James Crask
sec.
McKenney, Vincent & Jane Wilda Edwards 24 Sept. 1798, William
Edwards sec.
McKenney, William & Frances McKenney 19 Aug. 1791
McKenny, William & Caty Sanford 12 Jan. 1797, Gerard McKenny sec.
McKenney, William P. & Mary Young Hutt 13 Dec. 1849, Charles
C. Baker sec.

McKoy, Robert & Judith Day 7 July 1824, John T. Oldham sec.
McKoy, Roda & Agnes Douglass 15 Dec. 1842, Newton Burrell sec.

McKye, George & Hannah B. Aston 28 Oct. 1805, Steward R.
Pursell sec.

McKey, John & Margaret Spence 3 Mar. 1801, Uel Gilbert sec.

McNeil, Charles & Mary J. Brown 11 Apr. 1837, Samuel R. Thrift sec.

McNeil, John & Lucy Moxley - Not dated - Bundle marked "1807" John Davis sec.

Maddux, Thomas & Jane Middleton Crabb, Dau. John Crabb, 7 May 1793 John Crabb, Jr. sec.

Maiden, Daniel & Mary Johnson 10 Sept. 1828, Samuel Faucett sec.
Maiden, John & Mahailey Tate 7 Jan. 1828, Daniel Maiden sec.

Mann, Joseph & Sarah J. Pitts 30 Apr. 1850, Charles C. Baker sec.

Mariner, James & Lucy Weldon 5 May 1815, John Andrews sec.
Mariner, John H.R. & Martha Tete 28 Dec. 1842, William Pomroy sec.
Mariner, Richard N. & Ann Bispham 21 Dec. 1813, Samuel Templeman sec.
Mariner, Robert L. & Martha Mitchell 15 June 1843, Frederick Poor sec.
Mariner, Washington G. & Leanna Kew 25 Jan. 1812, Richard N. Mariner sec.

Marmaduke, Daniel & Nancy T. Dishman of the County of Loudon, now in the County of Westmoreland - Consent of Nancy T. Dishman dated 20 May 1808, Bond signed but not filled in - Robert Bispham sec.
Marmaduke, Daniel & Haney Curtice 8 June 1832, Joseph S. Lyell sec.
Marmaduke, John M. & Sarah Scales 8 Mar. 1827, William Hutt sec.
Marmaduke, Joseph & Judith Stone 31 Jan. 1798, William Luttrell sec.
Marmaduke, M. M. & Mary A. Porter 20 May 1846, John P. Norwood sec.
Marmaduke, Simpson & Mary Ann Jones 31 Jan. 1797, Samuel Templeman sec.
Marmaduke, Vincent & Betsy Blundell 26 Jan. 1803, William Marmaduke, Jr. sec.
Marmaduke, William & Martha Clark 25 Feb. 1797, John Grinnon sec.
Marmaduke, William & Polly Daffaul, dau. Vincent Daffaul(Duval?), Consent of Vinvent Daffaul dated 24 Dec. 1801, witnessed by Josiah Hazard, Bond signed but not filled in - Thomas Bland sec.
Marmaduke, William & Elizabeth Weaver, dau. Elizabeth Sanford, 9 Mar. 1843, Jacob V. Dolman sec.
Marmaduke, William B. & Catherine Quisenbury, dau. Jane Quisenbury, 27 Mar. 1837, N. Quisenbury sec.

Marks, Henry & Ann H. Mothershead, dau. Charles Mothershead, 26 Dec. 1832, James T. Jenkins sec.
Marks, Henderson & Verlinda Hammet 9 Mar. 1842, James F. Anderson sec.
Marks, John & Catherine Marks 15 Jan. 1821, Reuben Marks sec.
Marks, William & Betsy Jenkins 21 July 1806, John --- sec.

Marrow, Martin & Elizabeth Kirk, dau. John Kirk, 25 Dec. 1798,
    Reubin Spurling sec.

Marth, Jesse & Polly Jackson, dau. Elizabeth Jackson, 27 June,
    1803, Benedict Lamkin sec.

Marchant, John R. & Margaret N. Darnaby 10 Oct. 1835, David H.
    Chavis, Jr. sec.

Martin, Thomas & Elizabeth C. Payne 27 Nov. 1820, M. M. Marmaduke
    sec.

Marston, Henry & Sally Carrell 6 Jan. 1806, William M. Clark sec.

Mardas, William & Martha Mothershead 31 May 1837, William Sampson
    sec.

Maskiel, Henry & Jane Cary 31 Aug. 1816, Edward Birn sec.
Maskiel, Henry & Elizabeth Wroe 13 Sept. 1829, William Spurling
    sec.

Masse, Charles & Mary Wilson - Consent of Mary Wilson dated 11
    July 1822, Witnessed by Sarah & William Wilson - Bond
    signed but not filled in - William Wilson sec.
Massey, John & Elizabeth Kook 30 Nov. 1826, William B. Fleet sec.
Massey, Robert & Molley Jett 26 Mar. 1793, Thomas Jett sec.

Mathany, Daniel & Patty McClanahan 18 Jan. 1794, James Sutton sec.
Mathaney, Daniel & Eleanor Beane 14 Jan. 1819, Willis Garner sec.
Mathaney, George & Lucy A. Sutton 18 May 1826, William Sutton sec.
Mathaney, John & Winney Barecroft 9 Mar. 1787, Dan'l Laycock sec.
Mathany, Thomas & Mary W. Courtney 26 Apr. 1806, William Franklin
    sec.

Matthews, Philip & Nelly Hill - Not dated - Bundle marked "1822"
    James Carpenter sec.

Maxwell, Capt. John & Olivia Ann Mitchell 8 May 1809, John Smith
    sec.

Mayo, John & Mary L. Campbell 22 Apr. 1844, Robert Mayo sec.
Mayo, Robert & Emily Ann Campbell, dau. E. F. Campbell, 2 May
    1831, Joseph Jones sec.

Mazaro, Louis & Frances M. Gilbert 10 May 1819, John B. Yeatman
    sec.

Mealey, James & Polly Insley 21 Dec. 1826, Mottrom M. Wright sec.

Messick, John & Susan Kirck 25 Jan. 1806, Linsey Courtney sec.
Messack, Joseph & Nancy McNeil 4 June 1841, James S. Dozier sec.

Micon, Thomas H. & Lucinda James 8 June 1825, Thomas James sec.

Middleton, Benedict & Hannah Harrison 18 Sept. 1792, John
Middleton sec.
Middleton, George & Martha Atwell 12 Feb. 1791, Richard Bennett
sec.
Middleton, John & Hannah Wrow 29 Jan. 1788, George Middleton sec.
Middleton, Robert & Louisa H. Hall 25 May 1814, William Hall sec.
Middleton, William P. & Mary Morris 11 Feb. 1833, William Gilbert
sec.

Miller, Jacob & Lucinda Neale 15 Nov. 1815, Fielding Owens sec.
Miller, James & Peggy Hipkins 23 Dec. 1808, Robert G. Robb sec.
Miller, Richard & Adelaide T. Reamy 20 Feb. 1823, Thomas Miller
sec.
Miller, Spencer & Nancy S. Moxley 20 Dec. 1815, Reubin Briant sec.
Miller, Spencer & Mahala Morris 26 May 1817, Josiah Hazzard sec.
Miller, Spencer & Frances James 10 July 1820, O. H. Harvey sec.
Miller, Thomas & Jane McNeale 1 Jan. 1816, John Rodman sec.

Minor, Beverly & Lucinda B. McKenney 27 Apr. 1875, James McKenney
sec.
Minor, Elliott & Juliet Underwood 21 Dec. 1818, Henry Parker sec.

Mitchell, John & Roseanny Carpenter - Consent of John Carpenter
dated 28 Dec. 1803 - Bond signed but not filled in -
James Ryals sec.
Mitchell, Robert B. & Mary E. Peirce 17 Aug. 1829, Joseph
Peirce sec.
Mitchel, William & Susannah Muse 25 Dec. 1807, James Muse sec.

Montgomery, Andrew & Nancy Hall 17 July 1801, Robert Hall sec.
Montgomery, James & Elizabeth Hall 7 Nov. 1803, Andrew Montgomery sec.

Monroe, Elliott & Susannah Davis 1 Aug. 1795, William Redman sec.
Monroe, James L. & Rachel C. Smith, dau. William W. Smith, 18
Feb. 1822, John T. Smith sec.
Monroe, Jesse & Peggy Thornly 24 Oct. 1806, Joseph Fox sec.
Monroe, John & Betsey Triplett, dau. James Triplett, 10 Jan.
1797, Charles Triplett sec. - Badly damaged.

Monnett, Joseph & Jane Owen, dau. Ann Owen, 28 Dec. 1797, James
Bland sec.

Mooklar, William & Sally Attwell, dau. Mary Attwell, 20 Dec.
1791, William P. Tebbs sec.

Moon, Joseph & Rebecah Curtice 17 Dec. 1832, Daniel Marmaduke
sec.
Moone, Joseph H. & Sarah Elizabeth Short 19 May 1845, Frederick D. Alverson sec.

Moore, Charles S. & Ann Beale 17 June 1835, John H. Bailey sec.

Moore, George & Mary Sutton, dau. Richard Sutton, 2 April 1789
Thomas Sutton sec.

Moore, George & Hannah Smith, dau. John Smith - Consent of John
Smith dated 13 Dec. 1801, Witnessed by Willis Garner -
Bond signed but not filled in - Willis Garner sec.

Moore, John, son of Mary Ann Moore, & Ann Harris, dau. Elizabeth
Harris, 26 Mar. 1848, William Edmunds sec.

Moor, Reubin & Charlotte Thomas 25 Sept. 1792, Thomas Walker sec.

Moore, Stacks & Fanny Annandale 26 Dec. 1804, Vincent Jones sec.

Moore, Stephen & Sally Butler 11 Sept. 1792, Thomas Settle sec.

Moore, Vincent & (first name not filled in) Deatley 4 Jan. 1817,
Christopher Deatley sec.

Moore, Vincent & Polly Wroe 12 May 1818, William King sec.

Moore, William & Hannah Beale - Consent dated 18 Oct. 1809 -
Bond signed but not filled in - Jeremiah Thrift sec.

More, William & Sarah Garner 26 Aug. 1824, Samuel Anton sec.

Morgan, David & Elizabeth B. Lamkin 16 July 1816, William King
sec.

Morgan, Thomas & Susannah Burgess 19 May 1806, Harrison Burgess
sec.

Morton, John & Caty Mothershead 28 Nov. 1798, Nath'l Mothershead
sec.

Morris, Daniel & Betsey Sutton 10 Dec. 1801 - Bond signed but
not filled in - Jeremiah Sutton sec.

Morris, James & Sophia Dodd 21 Jan. 1824, Joshua Reamy sec.

Morriss, John & Elizabeth McKave 16 Apr. 1795, Joseph Dozier sec.

Morris, John & Elizabeth Ramey, dau. Benjamin Ramey, 2 Nov.
1821, Joshua Ramey sec.

Morris, John F. & Sarah Ann Montgomery, dau. Ann Montgomery, 21
Aug. 1833, Dempsey Porter sec.

Morris, William G. & Caty McKenney 9 May 1816, Presley McKenney
sec.

Morris, William K. & Fanny Guttridge 26 Feb. 1821, William
Guttridge sec.

Morris, William, Jr. & Mary Mothershead 15 Oct. 1828, Joshua
Reamy sec.

Morris, William & Ann G. Beacham 26 Apr. 1830, Jeremiah Middleton sec.

Morse, Ebenezer & Lucindey Carey 28 June 1819, Walter Self &
Willis Garner sec.

Morse, James & Frances Crabb 22 Jan. 1824, James King sec.

Morse, James & Mary Gawn 25 Dec. 1827, Dozier Garner sec.

Morse, Thomas & Ann Sisson 21 June 1792, Bailey Settle sec.

Moss, Obediah & Ann Self 17 Sept. 1788, Jeremiah Garner sec.

Moss, Thomas & Nancy Eidson 17 Jan. 1808, John Eidson sec.

Moss, Thomas & Mary Massey 7 Apr. 1828, Matthew Jenkins sec.

Moss, Thomas P. & Catherine G. Gawin, dau. Alice J. Gawin,
9 Dec. 1846, Joseph B. Thrift sec.

Mothershead, Brooks & Matilda Figget 14 Oct. 1802, William
Butler sec.
Mothershead, Charles & Kesiah Pendergrass 22 Dec. 1807, Richard
Efford sec.
Mothershead, Charles & Winneyfrid Jenkins 27 Nov. 1811, William
Doleman sec.
Mothershead, Charles & Susan Amanda Johnson 11 Mar. 1828, James
P. Jenkins sec.
Mothershead, Charles C. & Elizabeth Dozier 21 Dec. 1831, William
Johnson sec.
Mothershead, Christopher & Louisa Edmonds 9 May 1823, Vincent
Edmonds sec.
Mothershead, George & Lusey Green 26 Oct. 1799, George Deatly sec.
Mothershead, George G. & Catherine Crask 16 June 1814, Samuel
Mothershead sec.
Mothershead, George & Polly Howe, dau. Ann Howe, 7 Feb. 1815,
John Sandy sec.
Mothershead, George G. & Hannah C. Baber 15 Jan. 1816, William
G. Sturman sec.
Mothershead, Henry & Sally Weldon 29 Jan. 1816, Reubin Bryant
sec.
Mothershead, Henry & Eliza Rose 5 Feb. 1828, James Rose sec.
Mothershead, Humphrey & Jane E. Rose 29 May 1838, Matthew Deatly
sec.
Mothershead, James S. & Elizabeth Riley 30 Dec. 1799, Campbell
Teet sec.
Mothershead, James S. & Sally Riley 12 Feb. 1805, Campbell Teet
sec.
Mothershead, James & Jane Spilman 10 Apr. 1809, William Dolman
sec.
Mothershead, James H. & & Eliza Peed, dau. John Peed, 21 Dec.
1829, John Peed sec.
Mothershead, Jonn & Celia Massey 19 Aug. 1801, Thomas Massey
sec.
Mothershead, Richard & Margaret Muse 29 Dec. 1792, Newman Hall
sec.
Mothershead, Richard & Mary Stone 27 Dec. 1820, John Sutton sec.
Mothershead, Samuel & Margaret Kendall 19 Apr. 1808, William
Brennon sec.
Mothershead, Samuel & Elizabeth T. Richardson 16 Dec. 1814,
James Brewer sec.
Mothershead, Samuel & Elizabeth Dodd 22 Mar. 1820, Joseph Dodd
sec.
Mothershead, Stephen S. & Catherine Sampson 16 Oct. 1820, James
Sampson sec.
Mothershead, Thomas & Fanny Beddo 6 Feb. 1817, Samuel Mothers-
head, sec.
Mothershead, Thomas & Ann Brawner 24 May 1828, James Carpenter
sec.
Mothershead, William & Alice or Gary (consent signed by both)
Mothershead 17 Jan. 1809, James Mothershead sec.

Moxley, Alexander & Nancy Quisenbury, dau. Nicholas Quisenbury,
13 Jan. 1789, Rodham Moxley sec.

Moxley, Daniel & Fanny Branham 12 Feb. 1807, John Branham sec.
Moxley, Jeremiah & Hannah Morris 29 Jan. 1787, Rodham Moxley sec.
Moxley, Jeremiah & Hannah Robinson 23 May 1796, Solomon Robinson sec.
Moxley, Joseph & Caty Clayton 22 Oct. 1787, Richard Sanford sec.
Moxley, Richard & Sally Sisson 16 Mar. 1789, Martin Sisson sec.
Moxley, Richard & Ann R. Stone 22 Nov. 1841, James C. Harvey sec.
Moxley, Rodham & Mary Weldon 8 July 1810, Henry Lee sec.

Mozingo, John & Ruth Bragg 12 Jan. 1841, Thomas Mozingo sec.
Mozongo, Newton & Elizabeth Smith 22 Aug. 1821, William Johnson sec.
Mozingo, Peirce & Nancy Sutton 30 Sept. 1816, John Mozingo sec.
Mozingo, Richard & Nancy Yardly 10 May 1796, George Deatley sec.
Mozingo, Thomas & Mary Canniday 24 Sept. 1793, William Mozingo sec.

Mure, Charles S. & Elizabeth Elmore 1 Mar. 1841, Thomas T. Beale sec.
Muir, Charles & Margaret Williams 6 July 1816, Vincent T. Branson sec.
Muir, Charles S. & Jane E. Askins 3 July 1844, William Ticer sec.

Mullins, James H. & Lucy R. Fones 25 July 1842, Samuel R. Fones sec.
Mullins, John & Ruthey Barrett, dau. Elizabeth Jones, 14 June 1794, Reubin Sutton sec.
Mullins, John & Anna M. Weaver 3 Oct. 1806, Reubin Sutton sec.
Mullins, John H. & Mahala Ann Pursley, dau. John Pursley, 17 Jan. 1837, Presly Sanders sec.
Mullins, Spencer & Mary Brawner 2 Mar. 1803, John Brawner sec.
Mullins, Spencer & Jane Olliff 30 Dec. 1829, Samuel Olliff sec.

Mungar, Francis A. & Susanna Critcher 24 Sept. 1816, Robert B. Bailey sec.

Murphy, James B. & Susan B. Lowe 2 Sept. 1839, James Lowe sec.
Murphy, John & Anne Ballantine, dau. John Ballantine, 8 Nov. 1787, William Hutt sec. Badly damaged.
Murphy, John H. & Susan E. Smith 30 May 1843, John B. Murphy sec.
Murphy, Robert & Eliza B. Newton 18 May 1818, William L. Rogers sec.
Murphy, Robert & Mary Ann Jeffries, dau. Jeremiah Jeffries, 4 Jan. 1834, Enoch G. Jeffries sec.
Murphy, Robert W., of Montgomery, Alabama, & Frances A. Bailey, 22 Sept. 1846, William B. Bailey sec.
Murphy, William W. & Henrietta Parker 21 Apr. 1849, John T. Taliaferro sec.

Murray, John H. & Lucinda Weaver, dau. Elizabeth Sanford 23 May 1942, R. R. Hazard sec.

Murdock, William of King George County & Nancy Bristow, 4 Feb. 1788, Joseph Clapman sec.

Muse, Charles & Lucy Muse 2 July 1796, James Bland sec.
Muse, Charles & Catherine Jett 9 Feb. 1819, M. M. Marmaduke sec.
Muse, James A. & Elizabeth B. Walker 27 Jan. 1834, James H. Payne
sec.
Muse, Jessee & Rebecca Brown 10 Jan. 1810, Thomas Brown,Jr. sec.
Muse, John & Tabitha Gardner, wid., 16 June 1792, John Kew &
Thomas Newton Berryman sec.
Muse, John & Caty Davis 11 Sept. 1797, George Carter sec.
Muse, Nicholas & Anne Thompson, wid. 27 Jan. 1791, William W.
Smith sec.
Muse, Nicholas & Elizabeth Sanford 19 Nov. 1791
Muse, Reuben & Elizabeth Day 21 Jan. 1829, Samuel Day sec.
Muse, Samuel & Mary Arnol 24 June 1791, Augustine Smith sec.
Muse, Thomas & Lucinda Harvey 22 June 1820, Joseph Fox sec.
Muse, Thomas S. & Eliza M. Cox 13 Dec. 1841, Joseph S. Lyell sec.
Muse, Walker & Susanna Muse, wid. 9 Nov. 1790, Benjamin Hackney
sec.
Muse, William & Susan A. Berkley, dau. William Berkley, 19 June
1839, George Carter sec.

Nash, Alexander & Penelope Bartlett 31 Dec. 1806, Joseph Bartlett
sec.
Nash, George & Sally Mitchell - Not dated - Bond signed but not
filled in - George Field sec.
Nash, George & Ellin Dunnahew - Consent of Ellin Dunnahew not
dated - In bundle marked "1811" - Witnessed by Elizabeth
Dunnahew & William Reynolds.
Nash, James & Elizabeth Hill, dau. John & Elender Hill, 7 Sept.
1812, Elijah Knox sec.
Nash, James W. & Felicia White 4 Sept. 1816, Thomas Poor sec.
Nash, James & Martha Washington 28 Aug. 1823, Austin Hinson sec.
Nash, James L. & Margaret Short, dau. Jemimy Short, 9 Dec. 1848,
Joseph Hennage sec.
Nash, John, son of James Nash, & Molley Reynolds 14 Aug. 1794,
William Hunter sec.
Nash, Lewis & Sally Hinson dau. Meredith Hinson, 29 Dec. 1836,
O. E. P. Hazard sec.
Nash, Lewis & Milissa Gutridge 1 Jan. 1839, James Guttridge sec.
Nash, Ludwell & Sally Barnett 22 June 1813, John Redman sec.
Nash, Ludwell & Mary Sutton, 1 Sept. 1818, Elliott Stone sec.
Nathaniel Nash & Darcus Fryer, wid. 5 July 1791, Richard Brinn
sec.
Nash, Samuel & Sarah Green, dau. George Green, 6 Nov. 1843,
Charles Green sec.
Nash, Tarply & Elizabeth Gurgess - Not dated - In bundle marked
"1812" - William Burgess sec.
Nash, Thomas S. & Pattey Miller 27 Aug. 1818, Thomas Miller sec.
Nash, Thomas & Harriott Hinson 31 Dec. 1821, Campbell Tete sec.
Nash, Thornton & Alice Callahan 9 Nov. 1816, William King sec.
Nash, William & Elizabeth Spilman 14 Oct. 1794, George Nash sec.
Nash, William, of Richmond, & Caty Hinson of Richmond, dau. of
Nancy Hinson, 23 Jan. 1812, Reubin Marks & John Hinson sec.
Nash, William & Alice M. Mothershead 12 Feb. 1850, William L.
Mothershead sec.

Nash, Winder & Sally Alverson 7 June 1788, Teeleif Alverson sec.

Neale, John & Elizabeth Brewer 1 Sept. 1790, James Brewer sec.
Neale, John, Jr. & Margaret Miller 26 Oct. 1831, Richard Miller sec.
Neale, Joseph & Nancy Whearitt, wid. 28 Oct. 1794
Neale, Presley & Sally Jackson 21 Dec. 1786, James McNeil sec.
Neale, Presley S. & Elizabeth Carter 4 June 1834, Daniel Carter sec.
Neale, Richard & Mary Smith 16 Jan. 1800, George Field sec.
Neale, Rodham & Rose Smith 10 July 1805, John Strother sec.
Neale, Thomas & Patsey Hart 20 Dec. 1805, Charles Barnes sec.
Neale, Thomas P.W. & Shady Hinson 16 Sept. 1829, John Spilman sec.
Neale, William S. & Nancy Neale -- 1801, Presley Neale sec.

Nelson, William & Mary Harrison 31 Aug. 1791
Nelson, William & Jane Martin 10 Oct. 1796, Richard Thompson sec.
Nelson, William & Janney Martin, dau. Jacob Martin - Consent of
    Jacob Martin dated 10 Oct. 1796
Nelson, William & Ann E. Douglas 13 July 1814, John Turberville sec.
Nelson, William D. & Lettice E. Chandler dau. J. Chandler, 24
    Feb. 1841, David H. Tapscott sec.

Nelms, Edwin & Dianna Moss Omohundro 30 Aug. 1828, John Graham sec.

Newton, Isaac & Hannah Mathaney 4 May 1826, George Mathaney sec.
Newton, John P. & Mary E. Cox, sister of Fleet Cox, Consent of
    Fleet Cox dated 24 June 1822, Bond signed but not filled
    in - M. M. Marmaduke sec.
Newton, Willoughby & Sally Lee, wid. 23 May 1796, James Elliott sec.

Newman, Emanuel & Caroline Lucas 21 Dec. 1836, Richard Ashton sec.
Newman, Francis & Lawrendo Tate 27 Dec. 1847, Ewell Tate sec.
Newman, Frederick & Scilla Cary 30 Nov. 1813, Dennis Newman sec.
Newman, George & Lucy Buckley 29 Dec. 1812, Benjamin White sec.
Newman, Jacob & Juliet Tate 14 Feb. 1826, Edmond Tate sec.
Newman, Jacob & Isabella Sale 8 Apr. 1847, Hopeful Tate sec.
Newman, James & Jane Knott 24 Dec. 1806, Matthew Brann sec.
Newman, James & Sarah Fulcher 21 Feb. 1843, Samuel Howson sec.
Newman, James & Milly Bailey, dau. Fanny Bailey, 3 Feb. 1846,
    William H. Newman sec.
Newman, John & Nancy Griggs 3 Jan. 1844, Caphias Newman sec.
Newman, Samuel, a free black man & Jenny Johnson, a free black
    girl, 20 Mar. 1812, George Henry
Newman, Sephius & Fanny Johnson 2 Jan. 1833, Blain Ashton sec.
Newman, Thomas & Peggy Jett Bartlet 26 July 1791, Walter James sec.
Newman, Thomas & Peggy Bartlett 2 June 1801, Benjamin Simms sec.
Newman, Thomas & Lucy Johnson, a free black person, 26 July
    1819, George Weldon sec.

Newman, William H. & Malinda Lawrence, dau. Susanna Lawrence,
29 Feb. 1848, Ludwell Parker sec.

Northam, George H. & Elizabeth Walker 20 Mar. 1850, E. B.
Omohundro sec.

Northon, William & Lucy Yeatman 22 June 1801, George Field sec.

Norwood, John & Sally Brickley, dau. William Brickley - Consent
of William Brickley dated 28 Dec. 1801 - Bond signed
but not filled in - Joel L. Rose sec.
Norwood, John & Sally Porter dau. Edward Porter, 3 Nov. 1813,
Richard Croxton sec.

Nunn, Richard Q. & Catherine Carlton 20 Jan. 1817, Nathaniel
Crane sec.

Oharro, Thomas & Nancy Bunyan 20 Dec. 1810, Lawrence B. Fox sec.

Oldham, John T. & Elizabeth Morris 31 May 1825, George Delano
sec.
Oldham, Nathaniel & Martha Middleton, wid. 4 Apr. 1793, John
Middleton sec.

Ollive, James & Susannah Ollive 23 Mar. 1818, Elijah Ambrus sec.
Olive, James & Lucy Jones 29 Aug. 1825, Elijah Ambrose sec.
Olive, Reubin & Polly Head 18 Nov. 1806, John Pursley sec.
Olive, William & Rebecca Muse 11 June 1804, Burkett Muse sec.

Oliffe, Charles & Franky Davis Green, wid. 7 July 1789, William
Quisenbury sec.
Oliffe, Daniel M. & Mary Ann Mullins 26 Dec. 1832, Samuel Oliffe
sec.
Oliffe, Enoch & Eliza Ryall, dau. Sarah Oliffe, 28 Dec. 1831,
John L. Oliffe sec.
Oliffe, George & Mary Lanthrum 14 Apr. 1789, William Quisenbury
sec.
Oliff, Jessee & Bethuel Jenkins 13 May 1842, James Jenkins sec.
Oliff, John D. & Rebecca Scott 18 Apr. 1797, William Benson sec.
Oliff, John S. & Sary Ryals 25 May 1819, Benjamin R. Head sec.
Oliffe, Lofty & Susannah Jones 23 Aug. 1819, William Ballerson sec.
Oliffe, R. P. & Lucinda Moore 26 June 1843 Robert M. Gutridge sec.
Oliffe, Samuel & Sarah Ann Mullins ---- 17-- Elliott Stone sec.
Olliff, Thomas & Elizabeth Curtis - Consent of Elizabeth Curtis -
Not dated - Bundle marked "1811" - Witnessed by Jeremiah
Thrift.
Olliff, William & Eleanor Pullin 7 Dec. 1812, James Brown sec.
Olliffe, William & Ann Drake 1 June 1819, William Drake sec.

Omohundro, Edward B. & Sarah A. Reamy 1 July 1839, Steptoe T.
Rice sec.
Omohundro, John, son of William Omohundro, & Elizabeth Crask, dau.
Frances Crask, 8 May 1837, Jacob V. Doleman sec.

Omohundro, Richard F. & Mary B. Cloughton 29 Mar. 1839, Edward
    B. Omohundro sec.
Omohundro, Thomas & Nancy B. Blundell 16 Jan. 1808, Thomas
    Blundell sec.
Omohundro, Thomas & Sary P. Hunter 23 Dec. 1824, Charles Mothers-
    head sec.
Omohundro, William & Nancy Marmaduke 31 Jan. 1797, Thomas
    Omohundro sec.

Orsbourn, Michael & Charlott Clark -- 1823, G. G. Mothershead sec.

Otlay, James & Margaret Dickie - Consent of John Dickie dated
    5 June 1801 - Bond signed but not filled in - James
    Stroud sec.

Owens, Fielding & Polly Weeks, wid. 26 Aug. 1801, Thomas
    Wilkinson sec.
Owens, James, grandson of Elizabeth Owens,& Jane Simms 26 May
    1832, Benjamin Simms sec.
Owens, William W. & Elizabeth Simmes 24 Sept. 1832, Benjamin
    Simmes sec.

Packett, William & Ann Cooper 27 Jan. 1789, Henry Asbury sec.

Palmer, Thomas & Sarah Brown, dau. John Brown, 15 Feb. 1817,
    James Brown sec.
Palmer, William & Peggy Sanford 31 July 1790, James Rice sec.
Palmer, William & Rockey Jackson -- Sept. 1799, William Bowlin
    sec.
Palmer, William & Sarah Brinon 19 Dec. 1838, Thomas T. Beale sec.

Parker, Col. Alexander & Elizabeth Redmon, wid. 18 Mar. 1790,
    John Parker sec.
Parker, Henry & Elizabeth Downing 19 Mar. 1823, Richard T. Brown
    sec.
Parker, John & Elizabeth Muse 26 Jan. 1795, James Bland sec.
Parker, John A. & Louisa C. Forbes 9 Jan. 1826, John H. Peake sec.
Parker, Robert T. & Sarah Ann Williams, dau. William Williams,
    17 Dec. 1827, William Pursley sec.

Parks, Thomas D. & Susan Elmore 12 Oct. 1830, Enock G. Jeffries
    sec.
Parks, Thomas D. & Alice L. Jeffries 27 Feb. 1837, Robert Murphy
    sec.

Partridge, Matthew & Elizabeth B. Self 24 Mar. 1790, Moses Self
    sec.

Patrick, Richard T. & Polly Wheeler, dau. Richard Wheeler, 11
    Nov. 1841, Joseph H. Moone sec.

Peyton, Anthony & Betsy Hudnall 26 Jan. 1790, Birkett Jett sec.
Payton, John & Mary Weeks 19 Sept. 1798, John Payton sec.

Payton, William N. & Cordelia Bruce 28 June 1824, Edward Spence sec.

Payne, Daniel & Sarah Cox 15 Nov. 1815, Thomas Muse sec.
Payne, James & Ann Hunter 27 Dec. 1786, Rodham Mosley sec.
Payne, James & Anne Neale 18 Dec. 1798, Presley Neale sec.
Payne, John & Elizabeth Washington 28 Oct. 1805, Joseph Fox sec.
    Badly damaged
Payne, Meredith & Sarah Steward 7 Nov. 1811, Daniel Payne sec.

Peake, John H. & Elizabeth Parker 10 June 1823, Edward Spence sec.

Pearch, William & Nancy Thompson - Not dated - Bundle marked "1809"
    Bond signed but not filled in - Willoughby Thompson sec.

Pearson, John & Sarah Nevitt 8 July 1816, Henry Parker sec.

Peebles, Thomas A. & Elizabeth Pinckard 19 Feb. 1817, Henry P.
    Bowcock sec.

Peed, John & Jinny Guttridge, dau. Thomas Guttridge, 4 Dec. 1797,
    Elisha Newcombs sec.
Peed, John, Jr. & Sally Reamy 15 Sept. 1826, William J. Reamy sec.
Peed, William S. & Lucy Nash 19 May 1837, James H. Mothershead sec.
Peed, James & Caty Drake 15 Aug. 1809, John Peed & Presley Hinson
    sec.

Pegg, James & Elizabeth Hallbrooks 21 Jan. 1792, Thomas H.Moor sec.
Pegg, James & Mary Smith 31 May 1826, William Smith sec.
Pegg, Thomas & Harriott Bruce 13 Dec. 1807, Isaac Hall sec.

Peirce, Lovell & Patty Moxley 22 Jan. 1791, Richard Moxley sec.
Peirce, Lovell & Mary Ann Berkley, dau. William Berkley, 10 Aug.
    1823, John S. Carter sec.
Peirce, Ransdell & Nancy G. Barnes 28 Apr. 1847, William Hutt sec.
Peirce, William & Hannah Macoy 9 July 1828 Joseph Thompson sec.

Penn, Henry & Elizabeth Johnson 11 Mar. 1818, Thomas N. Berryman
    sec.

Perry, James & Sally Grinnan, dau. John Grinnan, 12 Feb. 1821,
    William ------- Damaged.

Pestuage, Beverly & Mary Ann Dean 18 Oct. 1836, Henry Cunningham
    sec.

Phillips, John & Mary Self 30 Apr. 1806, James Dunahoe sec.

Pick, Emanuel & Catherine Peake 22 May 1816, Richard T. Mitchell
    sec.

Pickett, Steptoe & Sarah O. Chilton 7 Jan. 1811, John Turberville
    sec.

Pillion, John & Cloey Allison 27 Feb. 1787, John Gawen sec.

Pilsbury, John & Sally Scott 26 Oct. 1787, James Peirce sec.
Pilsbury, John & Maria P. Butler 13 Feb. 1837, William B.Butler
    sec.
Pilsbury, Thomas & Maria Hall 21 Feb. 1824, Newyear C.Branson sec.

Pinstone, John & Martha Bragg, dau. Elizabeth Bragg, 22 Dec. 1790
    William Hall sec.

Piper, John & Jenny Fox, dau. Joseph Fox, 13 May 1788, John Jett
    sec.
Piper, William & Elizabeth Jett 9 July 1810, John Redman sec.

Pitts, Coleman & Nancy Dickerson 16 May 1812, William Rogers sec.
Pitts, George R. & C. E. Spence 3 May 1821, John H. Smith sec.

Pittman, Lee & Lottey Garner 7 Dec. 1795, James Bland sec.

Plummer, Thomas & Moley Middleton, wid. 7 Mar. 1795, Nathaniel
    Oldham sec.

Pomeroy, Esau & Elizabeth Green, dau. Charles Green - Consent of
    Charles Green dated 14 Sept. 1808 - Bond signed but
    not filled in - George Green sec.
Pomroy, William & Polly Johnson 4 Jan. 1832, Henry Teet sec.
Pomroy, William & Lucy Lucas 4 Mar. 1834, Walker Winkfield sec.
Pomeroy, William & Louisa Lucas, dau. Meredith Lucas, 12 May
    1837, Henry Winkfield sec.

Poor, Charles & Laurenda Mothershead, 8 May 1826, James Morris
    sec.
Poor, Frederick & Letty Weaver 14 May 1831
Poor, Frederick & Elizabeth Carpenter 1 Jan. 1839, Robert M.
    Gutridge sec.

Pope, Austin & Fanny Yeatman 7 Aug. 1793, William Luttrell sec.
Pope, Elliott & Mira Neale 26 Oct. 1826, John Bayne sec.
Pope, Henry W. & Ann Drake 3 Jan. 1832, B. Reamy sec.
Pope, John B. & Cynthia Annodale 30 Sept. 1815, Charles C. Rice
    sec.
Pope, John & Susan McCluskey 11 June 1834, James K. Johnson sec.
Pope, Lawrence & Frances Carter 30 Dec. 1790, William Edwards
    sec.
Pope, Lawrence & Peney Vigar, wid., 22 Nov. 1793, Austin Pope
    sec.
Pope, Laurence B. & Rockey Grinnan, dau. John Grinnan, 12 Feb.
    1821, John Bayne sec.
Pope, William & Penny Annadale, wid. 5 Sept. 1792, Christopher
    Deatley sec.

Porter, Benjamin & Polly Templeman 16 Feb. 1804, Samuel Templeman
    sec.
Porter, David & Lucy B. Atwill 13 Feb. 1839, David Atwill sec.
Porter, Edward & Mary McClanahan 7 Jan. 1789, William Porter sec.

Porter, Edward & Mary Montgomery, dau. Andrew Montgomery, 23
May 1822, M. M. Marmaduke sec.
Porter, Edward & Tiffey (sic) 12 Apr. 1824, Thomas S. Davis sec.
Porter, Elliott & Frances Edwards, dau. Frankey Edwards, 5 Feb.
1807, Dozier Lyell sec.
Porter, John & Patty Sisson 10 Apr. 1795, John Gordon sec.
Porter, Thomas S. & Ann Linthecum 1 Mar. 1827, Austin Dozier sec.
Porter, Thomas T. & Olivia Harris 11 Dec. 1828, John H.Peake sec.
Porter, William & Mary Sandy, dau. Uriah & Anne Sandy, 27 May
1768, Edward Porter sec.
Porter, William & Amanda C. Baber 11 Nov. 1823, George G.
Mothershead sec.

Potter, John & Margarett Hawkins, wid. 7 Nov. 1787, James Lamkin
sec.
Potter, John & Elizabeth Newman 15 Jan. 1814, William Butler sec.
Potter, John & Polly Butler 1 Jan. 1816, William Johnson sec.
Potter, Reubin & Ellen Briscoe 26 Sept. 1800, Reubin Briscoe sec.
Potter, Reubin & Lucy Fawbush 26 July 1815, Samuel Bromley sec.
Potter, William & Ann M. McKinney 16 Apr. 1829, Thomas Cose sec.

Potts, Richard, Jr. & Martha Willson 5 June 1804, Henry Wilson
sec.

Pound, William H. & Martha Green, dau. George Green, 17 Aug. 1749
Samuel Nash sec.

Power, John & Elizabeth Reynolds 19 June 1815, Samuel Gilbert sec.
Powers, John & Eliza Ann Montgomery 30 July 1828, Stephen D.Pitts
sec.

Powell, John N. & Mary C. Wright 24 Jan. 1842, William Hutt sec.

Pratt, James & Alcy Oliff 12 Apr. 1815, Elijah Oliff sec.
Pratt, James & Fanny Jenkins 10 Apr. 1821, James Olive sec.

Prim, Kitchen & Mary Clark 13 Jan. 1787, James Wiggly sec.

Pridham, William R. & Sally Morris 11 Feb. 1833, William Morris
sec.
Pridham, William R. & Mary Smith, dau. W. R. Smith, 29 Nov. 1844,
Samuel B. Hardwick sec.

Pritchet, Henry & Alice R. Sanford 7 Jan. 1825, William McGuire
sec.
Pritchet, Richard & Felitia Lune (sic) 23 Oct. 1824, James S.
Rice sec.
Pritchett, Zachariah & Peggy Chilton, dau. William Chilton, 20
Apr. 1804, Samuel Baker sec.

Pullin, Andrew & Rebecca Wilson 7 Mar. 1804, James Scales sec.
Pullin, John & Hany Bowen, dau. Thomas & Mary Bowen, 9 Oct.
1827, Smith Ginnings sec.

Pursley, James & Sarah Green 10 Nov. 1801 - Consent of Sarah
Green - Bond signed but not filled in - Charles Bettisworth sec.

Pursley, James & Susan Eidson 27 Feb. 1838, Lewis P. Steel sec.

Pursley, Jesse & Winney Yardley - Not dated - Bundle marked "1801"
Bond signed but not filled in - William Harrison sec.

Pursley, John & Sarah Washington - Not dated - Bundle marked
"1800" - William Nash sec.

Pursley, John & Katharine Barker 22 Dec. 1837, William S. Peed
sec.

Pursly, Meredith & Jane Nash 27 Aug. 1827, James Eidson sec.

Pursley, Ottoway & Jane Ellen Combs 25 Dec. 1848, Henry Combs
sec.

Pursley, Rolley & Delilah Edmonds 14 Jan. 1834, Uriah E. Head sec.

Pursley, Thomas & Elizabeth Riels 19 May 1796, John Hill sec.

Pursley, William & Ann Margaret Wilkins 1 Apr. 1830, James Peed
sec.

Pursell, Benjamin & Margaret Templeman, dau. Samuel Templeman,
24 Dec. 1834, John H. McClanahan sec.

Pursell, Hiram M. & Hannah L. Middleton dau. Jeremiah Middleton,
26 Jan. 1841, Samuel W. English sec.

Purcell, Hudson & Fanny Mothershead, 24 years of age, 3 June,
1796, James Adkins sec.

Pursell, Philip & Mary Templeman dau. Samuel Templeman, 5 Jan.
1835, Robert H. P. Crabb sec.

Pursell, Stephen D. & Elizabeth S. Chevis 28 Jan. 1839, William
Hutt sec.

Purley, John & Elizabeth Carter 31 Aug. 1816, John Carter sec.

Putnam, John G. & Sarah Lewis 20 Oct. 1838, William Hutt sec.

Quisenbury, George & Jane Carter Pope 27 Nov. 1809, John H.
Doleman sec.

Quisenbury, Joseph & Charlotte White 18 Aug. 1828, James Morris
sec.

Quisenbury, Richard & Lucy Mothershead 21 May 1835, Charles
Mothershead sec.

Quinton, Hugh & Anne Tasker Peck 20 Apr. 1796, James Bland sec.

Quinton, Hugh & Judith Brereton Thompson 23 Aug. 1803, Martin
Tapscott sec.

Ramey, John & Mary McGuire 24 Dec. 1821, William Sutton sec.

Ramey, Richard R. & Liza J. Barrack 11 Apr. 1846, Stephen Owens
sec.

Randall, John & Sally Barrott 6 June 1821, James Weaver sec.
Badly damaged.

Reamy, Albert J. & Mahala M. Mathis, dau. Prissey Mathis, 29
    Dec. 1823, Thomas Miller sec.
Reamy, George W. H. & Elizabeth Hutt 25 Jan. 1836, Joseph F.
    Harvey sec.
Reamy. James & ------------- 23 Dec. 1811, John Neale sec.
Reamy, James & Lucy Brewer 25 Nov. 1817, James Brewer sec.
Reamy, John N.,son of Beriman Reamy, & Jane Peed, dau. of John
    Peed, 15 Dec. 1834, Samuel T. Reamy sec.
Reamy, Joshua & Meriah Neale, dau. John Neale, 22 June, 1814,
    William W. Neale sec.
Reamy, Joshua & Fanny Morris 31 Aug. 1818, Daniel Morris sec.
Reamy, Milton & Fanny Sampson 18 Mar. 1839, Sylvanus Simpson sec.
Reamy, Samuel T.,son of Beriman Reamy, & Susan C. Fones 25 Apr.
    1832, Joshua Reamy sec.
Reamy, William J. & Catherine Morris, dau. Sally Mothershead,
    wife of William Mothershead, 26 Mar. 1827, Joseph Reamy
    sec.

Read, Joseph & Polly Wigley 31 Oct. 1805, James Wigley sec.
Read, Richard & Betsey Washington 22 Sept. 1794, Thomas Muse sec.
Read, Simon & Frankey Weldon 9 Nov. 1824, Lisha Weldon sec.

Reade,Stephen & Nancy S. Dozier 14 Oct. 1815, Allen S. Dozier

Reed, Andrew & Martha Nash 4 June 1835, William Sutton sec.
Reed, Colev & Frances Clark 22 Dec. 1834, Richard Omohundro sec.
Reed, Colev & Lucy Sanfora 20 May 1837, William Tallent, Jr. sec.
Reed, Edwin G. & Mary L. Crask 24 Dec. 1838, Williamson Hall sec.
Reed, George & Delia Gutridge 2 Apr. 1850, George Deatley sec.
Reed, John & Kitty M. Kelly 28 Nov. 1822, Richard Reed sec.
Reed, John, son of George Reed & Ann Lamkin 27 July 1835, Milton
    A. Harvey sec.
Reed, William, son of George Reed, & Sally Sampson, dau. Molly
    Sampson, 31 Dec. 1825, Joseph F. Harvey sec.
Reed, William & Harriet Gaskins 6 Aug. 1831, Henry Johnson sec.
Reed, William B. & Jane E. Deatley 23 Mar. 1839, Matthew
    Deatley sec.

Redman, John & Alice Deatley 18 Sept. 1812, George Deatley sec.
Redman, John & Eliza Palmer, dau. William Palmer, 23 Jan. 1826,
    Benedict Johnson sec.
Redman, Solomon & Frances Robinson 11 May 1799, Willis Garner
    sec.
Redman, Solomon & Sally A. Robinson 25 Apr. 1821, Thomas Stowell
    sec.
Redman, William & Elizabeth Shoats 24 Feb. 1795, William Benson
    sec.
Redman, William & Frances Carter 11 Aug. 1821, William A. Butler
    sec.

Rennolds, Arthur F. & Susan N. Jett 24 July, 1837, Benjamin F.
    Stewart sec.
Reynolds, Carroway & Susan Ann Weaver 31 Dec. 1842, James A.
    Weaver sec.

Reynolds, Conway & Harriett A. McKenny 7 Feb. 1850, James
McKenny sec.
Reynolds, Joseph & Martha McKenney, dau. Reubin McKenney, 16
Dec. 1834, William R. McKenney sec.
Reynolds, Reubin & Elizabeth Thomas 5 Sept. 1804, William Rey-
nolds sec.
Reynolds, Vincent & Winney Brickey 13 Oct. 1797, William Brickey
sec.
Reynolds, Vincent & Hadassah Hazzard - Consent of Hadassah
Hazzard dated 22 Nov. 1803, Bond signed but not filled
in - William Hazard sec.
Reynolds, Vincent & Frances Sisson 15 Dec. 1806, John Sisson sec.
Reynolds, William & Hannah Morton 24 Dec. 1793, James Hawkins
sec.
Reynolds, William & Lorinda Reynolds 24 Dec. 1842, James Rey-
nolds sec.

Rich, Daniel & Catherine Lewis 9 Apr. 1836, John Hunter sec.
Rich, Lindsey & Phelicia Tate 3 Jan. 1837, Simon Tate sec.

Richards, John S. & Nancy Mozingo 2 Mar. 1842, John Mozingo sec.
Richards, John P. & Sarah S. Peck 20 Feb. 1850, William B.
Mitchell sec.
Richards, Reuben & Elizabeth McGuire, dau. William McGuire, 29
Jan. 1833, Christopher B. Mozingo sec.

Richardson, James & Nancy Dishman, dau. John Dishman, 10 Aug.
1787, James Bland sec.
Richardson, Mourning & Byron Triplett 12 July 1799, John P.
Hungerford sec.

Rice, Caleb & Sabinah Riggs 14 Mar. 1804, Thomas R. Sanford sec.
Rice, Charles & Elender Lord Smith 9 Jan. 1809, William Hazzard
sec.
Rice, James & Jemima Spence 1 Jan. 1789, Thomas Spence sec.
Rice, James & Margaret Brown 31 Jan. 1821, John Brown sec.
Rice, John T. & Mary C. Robinson 29 Aug. 1831, William M.
Dameron sec.
Rice, John & Jane H. Hall 10 Dec. 1833, Levi Barnett sec.
Rice, Steptoe T. & Frances M. Robinson 25 Dec. 1843, Thomas S.
Rice sec.
Rice, Thomas & Letty A. Stowers, dau. Thomas Stowers, 12 May
1817, Solomon Rodman sec.
Rice, Thomas B. & Naney R. Redman 19 Feb. 1819, John Redman sec.

Riddles, John & Sally Head, dau. Isaac & Rachel Head, 28 Sept.
1812, Marshall B. Head sec.

Right, John W. & Mary Tompson 12 Aug. 1844, Bennet Thompson sec.

Rigg, Jonathan & Catherine Quizenbury, dau. Nicholas Quizenbury,
22 Feb. 1794, John Eskridge sec.

Riley, Henry A. & Sarah Tiffey 6 Dec. 1820 -

Roane, Thomas T. & Mary Vaughan, dau. Walter Vaughan, 20 Jan.
1834, James M. Vaughan sec.

Robb, Robert G. & Eve Bankhead 1 Mar. 1808, Joseph Fox sec.

Robinson, Beverly & Sally Cox 25 Jan. 1803, Martin Tapscott sec.
Robinson, James & Sally A. Crenshaw, dau. David Crenshaw, Con-
sent of David Crenshaw dated 27 Dec. 1812 - Witnessed by
John Crenshaw.
Robinson, John & Elizabeth Davis, dau. Elias Davis, 12 Nov. 1793
James Rowles sec.
Robinson, John & Mary A. Pursell 5 June 1839, C^t Robinson sec.
Robinson, Porter & Mary P. Wright 29 July 1843, Benedict Walker
sec.
Robinson, Solomon & Frances Redman 13 Mar. 1797, William Redman
sec.
Robinson, Thomas R. & Jemima Mathews 14 May 1796, Thomas Prit-
chett sec.
Robinson, Thomas & Kesiah Seader (?) 24 Nov. 1798, William
Robinson sec.
Robinson, William & Nancy Washington 8 Oct. 1800, William Aug^t
Washington sec.
Robinson, William & Sally McKinney 13 Mar. 1802, Gerrard
McKinney sec.
Robinson, William D. & Sarah Richardia Cox 7 Sept. 1824, George
R. Pitts sec.
Robinson, William B. & Ann M. Wright 29 Feb. 1836, William R.
McKenney sec.

Robertson, Oscar F. & Eliza P. Claughton 23 July 1838, P. C.
Claughton sec.
Robertson, Thomas W. N. & Lucy F. Harvey 2 Mar. 1844, James C.
Harvey sec.
Robertson, William & Elizabeth Jeffries 21 Feb. 1798 (Bond not
signed) James Newton sec.

Rochester, Jeremiah & Molley F. Northern - Consent of Mary F.
Northern dated 12 May 1808 - Bond signed but not filled
in - William Richards & John Sanford sec.

Rockwell, Seth & Patty Atwell 21 Jan. 1822, Thomas T. Atwell sec.

Roe, John & Ann Monroe, dau. Elizabeth Monroe, 12 June 1787,
Henry Roe sec.
Roe, John & Elizabeth Coats 4 Jan. 1823, William Carter sec.

Rogers, Benjamin & Susannah Weaver 3 Nov. 1798, Thomas Claxton sec.
Rogers, John M. & Eliza J. Murphy 1 Nov. 1843, Robert Murphy sec.

Rogers, William L. & Ann Ballantine Murphy, dau. John Murphy,
16 July 1816, Robert Murphy sec.

Roles, James & Molly Robinson, dau. Sarah Robinson, 2 June 1789,
Brown Robinson sec.

Rollins, James & Fanny Lucas 20 Aug. 1845, Elliott Lucas sec.

Roper, George E. & Mary Sutton, dau. Frances Sutton, 18 Oct.
1821, John McPherson sec.

Rose, Alexander F. & Mildred W. Rose 20 Feb. 1810, William Robin-
son sec.
Rose, Bennett & Elizabeth Hutchings 27 Sept. 1797, William L.
Hutchings sec.
Rose, Bennett & Nancy Brickley, dau. William Brickley, 28 Mar.
1803, John Norwood sec.
Rose, Bennett & Agnes Barber 19 Dec. 1807, Joel S. Rose sec.
Rose, Bennett & Sally 3. Sels, dau. William Self, 8 Jan. 1811,
James Lamkin sec.
Rose, Dr. Henry & Ann Washington Robinson 19 Nov. 1795, Aug: J.
Smith sec.
Rose, Joel S. & Frances Weaver 28 Dec. 1795, John Rose sec.
Rose, Joel L. & Frankey Rice - Consent of Frankey Rice dated 10
Feb. 1802, Witnessed by Elizabeth Brinnon & Hannah
Norwood - Bond signed but not filled in - Bennett Rose sec.
Rose, John & Nancy Lamkin 15 Dec. 1792, Francis Rose sec.
Rose, John & Sebinah Collinsworth 12 Oct. 1795, Stephen Moore sec.
Rose, John & Mary Bennett 22 Feb. 1827, James Rose sec.
Rose, Willis & Jane E. Redman 23 July 1834, Charles H. Sanford sec.

Rowles, James & Nancy Cavender 11 Mar. 1815, James Crask sec.
Rowles, William & Nancy Crask 12 Dec. 1826, Thomas Edwards sec.

Rowland, Thomas R. & Elizabeth A. Connellee, dau. Elizabeth S.
Connallee, 21 Aug. 1838, William H. Hill sec.

Roy, James & Nancy Washington, dau. Const: Washington, 6 Dec.
1790, Thomas Lund Washington sec.

Rust, Benedict & Elizabeth Middleton 4 Jan. 1797, Benedict Crabb
sec.
Rust, George & Elizabeth Dunbar, wid. 28 Oct. 1786, James Rust
sec.
Rust, George & Ursla P. Robinson 16 May 1806, Dozier Lyell sec.
Rust, James Newton & Peggy Courtney 21 Feb. 1798, William
Robertson sec. - Bond not signed.
Rust, Peter & Elizabeth Ball Downman 28 Dec. 1793, John Cloughton
sec.
Rust, Peter N. & Polly Morse 23 Dec. 1811, George Smith sec.
Rust, Samuel & Sary Clanahan 21 Feb. 1798, William Robertson sec.
Badly damaged

Ryals, James & Elizabeth Brennon 15 Oct. 1801, John Morton sec.

Ryals, William & Elizabeth Carter --1806, James Ryals sec.

Sabastian, John H. & Ann A. Barock 17 May 1845, George G. Barock
sec.

Sadler, Thornton M. & Sarah A. Lamkin 19 Aug. 1844, Richard E.
Deatley sec.

Sampson, Jemerson & Sary Ann Oliff 10 Apr. 1827, Stephen S.
Mothershead sec.
Sampson, Sylvanus & Anne Deatley, dau. Christopher Deatley, 17
Apr. 1822, William Deatley sec.
Sampson, William & Ann Barker 8 June 1836, James Sampson sec.

Samson, William & Lucy Stephens 3 Feb. 1846, John Deacons sec.

Sandy, Thomas & Anne Lewis, wid. 16 Mar. 1792, John Brown, Jr.
sec.
Sandy, Thomas & Isabella Beale 28 Sept. 1815, Thomas Barber sec.
Sandy, Thomas & Alethea Brann 16 Dec. 1817, Joseph Harrison sec.
Sandy, Vincent & Elizabeth Reynolds 18 Jan. 1838, Baldwin B.
McKenney sec.

Sanford, Augustine & Jemima Sanford 28 May 1796, William Hazard
sec.
Sanford, Augustine, Jr. & Sebey Mozingo 31 Nov. 1820, George R.
Pitts sec.
Sanford, Charles & Betty Porter 28 May 1792, Presley Stone sec.
Sanford, Charles & Sabina Rose 22 Sept. 1800, Thomas Claxton sec.
Sanford, Daniel & Susanna Sanders 22 May 1797, Edward Stone sec.
Sanford, Daniel & Rutho McGinniss 13 July 1803, John Hunter sec.
Sanford, Daniel & Mary Weaver 15 Sept. 1812, James Anthony sec.
Sanford, Edward & P----ty Teatman 24 Nov. 1787, Robert Sanford
sec. - Badly damaged.
Sanford, Edward T. & Lydia Boothe 17 Dec. 1834, Presley McKenney
sec.
Sanford, Elijah & Peggy Sanford 30 Aug. 1811, John Dodd sec.
Sanford, Gerard A. & Sebina B. Jenkins 18 Oct. 1820, M. M. Marma-
duke sec.
Sanford, Henry & Ann Johnson, dau. Matthias Johnson, 22 Oct.
1833, Joseph B. Reed sec.
Sanford, Henry P. & Mary Ann Hall 3 Mar. 1845, Samuel P. Harrison
sec.
Sanford, James & Elizabeth Weaver 6 Nov. 1834, James P. Jenkins
sec.
Sanford, James & Olivia Withers 2 Jan. 1844, Samuel J. Booth sec.
Sanford, Jeremiah & Harriot Weaver - Consent of Harriot Weaver
dated 28 Oct. 1809, Witnessed by John McNeil, Bond
signed but not filled in - John McNeil sec.
Sanford, John & Dianna McKenny, dau. George McKenny, dec., 28
Dec. 1796, Gerard McKenny sec.
Sanford, John & Harriot Morrison 17 Jan. 1818, Charles D. Scutt
sec.

Sanford, John H. & Susan Bailey, dau. Ann P. Bailey, 15 Apr. 1845
Robert B. Jett sec.

Sanford, Joshua & Lucy Wilson 7 Oct. 1814, Armstrong McKenney sec.

Sanford, Lawrence M. & Mary J. Beale, dau. William L. Beale, 14
Mar. 1813, Willis Garner sec.

Sanford, Lewis & Leannah Bayne 14 Apr. 1838, Elliott Pope sec.

Sanford, Lewis & Lovinda Sanford 12 Mar. 1839, Joseph T. Harvey
sec.

Sanford, Meredith & Eliza Sanford 13 Feb. 1826, William L.
Sanford sec.

Sanford, Patrick S. & Hannah Butler 30 Oct. 1818, Francis Self
sec.

Sanford, Reubin & Ann Washington 11 Dec. 1799, William Dolman
sec.

Sanford, Roubin & Judah Saunders 26 Jan. 1809, John Saunders sec.

Sanford, Reubin & Mary Wilson 4 Nov. 1812, David Sanders sec.

Sanford, Richard & Hannah Sutton 11 Aug. 1795, Thomas Dolman sec.

Sanford, Richard H. & Amelia Mothershead, dau. Sally Mothershead
24 Oct. 1832, Henry H. Hazard sec.

Sanford, Richard & Eliza S. Walker 21 June 1833, William W. Brown
sec.

Sanford, Richard & Eliza Garner 14 Mar. 1838, Willis P.Garner sec.

Sanford, Robert & Sally Newton 8 Jan. 1789, Edward Sanford sec.

Sanford, Robert & Aggay Hazard 1 Feb. 1797, Edward Sanford sec.

Sanford, Robert & Sally R. Clarke, dau. Jeremiah Clarke, 15 Apr.
1801, William J. Neale sec.

Sanford, Robert & Susannah Fox 20 July 1807, Joseph Fox sec.

Sanford, Robert & Mahala Miller 24 July 1837, Granville White sec.

Sanford, Robert & Mary Riley 22 Sept. 1841, Rodney Moxley sec.

Sanford, Rodaham & Minerva J. Mothershead 20 Dec. 1824,
Mourning Harris sec.

Sanford, Thomas & Frances Brown 22 Aug. 1798, John Davis sec.

Sanford, Thomas & Adeline Reamy 15 Feb. 1834, William Johnson sec.

Sanford, William & Ann Spence 24 Jan. 1774

Sanford, William S. & Elizabeth Yeatman 27 May 1799, John Gordon
sec.

Sanford, William & Ellin Dolman - Consent of Mary McNeil &
Elender Dolman dated 7 July, 1802 - Bond signed but not
filled in - John Davis sec.

Sanford, William & Sarah Hallbrooks 23 Nov. 1818, Spencer Mullins
sec.

Sanford, William H. & Mary S. Moxley 7 June 1819, George R.
Weldon sec.

Sanford, William J. & Fanny Holbrook 12 Aug. 1830, Thomas M.
Belfield sec.

Sanford, William H. & Mary E. Cox 27 Jan. 1845, Walter Bowie sec.

Sandford, Anderson, & Lucy Clarke 3 Apr. 1821, John M. Luttrell
sec.

Sandford, Ethelwald & Sally M. Robinson 29 May 1819, Thomas S.
Muse sec.

Sandford, Robert & Eliza B. Harvey, dau. John Harvey, 10 Sept.
1817, Henry Hungerford sec.

Sandford, William & Nancy Bain 11 Mar. 1828, Samuel Sandy sec.

Sanders, Allen & Martha F. Newman 27 Dec. 1814, Dan'l Sanders sec.
Sanders, Charles & Elizabeth Watson 21 Oct. 1789, Joseph Sanders
    sec.
Sanders, Daniel & Mary Bragg 6 Mar. 1803, William Sanders sec.
Sanders, James & ----- Carpenter -- Jan. 1808, James Carpenter sec.
Sanders, James & Felicia Fisher 13 Jan. 1818, Daniel Saunders sec.
Sanders, James & Felicia Tallent 21 Oct. 1847, Alexander Carpen-
    ter sec.
Sanders, John & Nancy Frame, dau. John & Caty Frame, -- 1807,
    Samuel Ryals sec.
Sanders, John & Margaret Tiler 22 Mar. 1820, George Reed sec.
Sanders, Richard & Mary Ann Smither 14 July 1799, Edmund Terrill
    sec.
Sanders, Robert & Susannah Drake 25 Mar. 1818, John Drake sec.
Sanders, Thomas & Bartlet Jones 19 Dec. 1807, Charles Fones sec.
Sanders, William & Mary Peed 15 Jan. 1793, Aleck Sanders sec.
Sanders, William T. & Frances Weaver 25 Jan. 1802, Thomas Poor
    sec.
Sanders, William & Anne Playl 18 Sept. 1803, William Sanders sec.
Sanders, William & Sukey Marks, dau. James & Frances Marks, 22
    May 1815, Jonas Hinson sec.
Sanders, William & Mary Burges 22 Sept. 1819, John Burges sec.
Sanders, Zachariah & Margaret A. Oliffe 9 Dec. 1844, James S.
    Weaver sec.

Saunders, George & Frances Jennings 23 Dec. 1847, Washington
    Scales sec.
Saunders, James L. & Peggy Marks 28 Feb. 1825, James Jenkins sec.
Saunders, James & Sally Hinson 29 Dec. 1830, Henry Sanders sec.
Saunders, James & Jane S. Mothershead -- Apr. 1848, William L.
    Mothershead sec.
Saunders, John & Catharine Tallent 16 June 1829, John Burgess sec.
Saunders, John & Mary Reamey dau. Berryman Reamey,1 Jan. 1838,
    Samuel Reamy sec.
Saunders, Presley & Fanny L. Tallant 11 Jan. 1842, James H.
    Tallant sec.
Saunders, William Alexander & Mary E. Monroe, 28 Sept. 1829,
    Richard Monroe sec.

Scales, Bartlett & Susanna Bartlett 7 Oct. 1807, John Bartlett sec.
Scales, Elijah & ---- Newman 22 Feb. 1808, George Newman sec.
Scales, James & Frances Thomas 25 Jan. 1838, James H. Muse sec.
Scales, Joseph R. & Julia A. Stone 14 Jan. 1848, James H. Reed sec.
Scales, Washington & Elizabeth Reynals 17 Dec. 1838, Thomas
    Anthony sec.

Scoonover, John & Fanny Drake 18 Feb. 1806, Richard H.Simms sec.

Scoot, William & Nelly Mozingo 12 Aug. 1845, Thomas Mozingo sec.

Scott, Charles & Rebecca McClanahan 14 Mar. 1807, James Jewell sec.
Scott, Charles & Fanny Newman 13 July 1808, Vincent Edmonds sec.

Scrimsher, William & Frances Sanford 11 Dec. 1793, Daniel Sanford
sec.

Scutt, John & Fanny Sanford 21 Jan. 1817, John Sanford sec.
Scutt, Thomas & Molly Howell 9 Aug. 1813, John Scutt & Thomas
Barber sec.
Scutt, William & Maria Bartlet 7 Jan. 1829, Henry Mothershead sec.

Scurlock, George & Milly Self 29 Oct. 1798, Nath'l Oldham sec.

Sedwick, George & Sally Hall 15 Aug. 1806, Andrew Montgomery sec.

Seettle, William & Nancy King, dau. Thomas King, 15 July 1821,
Joseph Fox sec.

Selby, Ebenezer & Nancy Brown 17 Feb. 1805, William Beddo sec.
Selby, Joseph & Nancy Ambrose 1 Jan. 1807, James Hinson sec.

Selvy, Ebenezer & Sara Deatley 13 Feb. 1818, James Brown sec.

Self, Francis & Ann Thrift 20 Sept. 1806, Job Self sec.
Self, James & Maria Elmore 19 Dec. 1825, Enoch G. Jeffries sec.
Self, Job & Sarah Anton, dau. Rebecca Johnson, 17 Nov. 1831,
Thomas Sardy sec.
Self, James C. & Deborah Garner 10 Apr. 1795, Obediah Moss sec.
Self, Lunsford & Elizabeth Messick 28 Dec. 1825, Enoch G. Jeff-
ries sec.
Self, Moses, Jr. & Mary S. Smith, dau. Peter Smith, 5 Jan. 1826
Jeremiah Middleton sec.
Self, Moses & Ann Crask 13 Jan. 1831, Jacob V. Doleman sec.
Self, Moses & Sally Crask 22 Dec. 1834, Jacob V. Doleman sec.
Self, Peter S. & Susan R. Garner 31 Mar. 1838, Job Self sec.
Self, Robert & Jane E. Kirk, dau. Sarah Kirk, 13 Oct. 1847,
William Carey sec.
Self, Samuel B. & Eliza M. Self 5 July 1843, Peter L. Self sec.
Self, Stephen & Eliza Lewis 29 Dec. 1830, Daniel Hardwick sec.
Self, Walter D. & Lucy S. Brann 15 Apr. 1845, Robert M. Self sec.
Self, William & Jemima Partridge, wid. 6 Sept. 1788, Moses Self
sec.
Self, William & Polly Kent 20 Jan. 1811, Jeremiah Thrift sec.
Self, William & Elizabeth Lambert 21 Dec. 1816, William McKildoe
sec.
Self, William Henry & Elizabeth Jane Ticer, dau. William Ticer,
7 Dec. 1847, Joseph B. Thrift sec.
Self, Youel & Ann Walker 26 Dec. 1789, Thomas Walker sec.

Settle, William & Mary Greenlow 8 Aug. 1798, Richard Redman sec.

Shackleford, John & Martha Newman 20 Jan. 1842, Fleet Gregory sec.

Sherley, William & Cloe Merchant 24 Dec. 1793, William Reynolds
sec.

Short, Alford & Sally Cracy 25 Apr. 1845, William Morran sec.

Short, Benjamin & Mary J. J. Crabb 19 Dec. 1848, Richard Dozier sec.
Short, Clark & Nancy Alverson 9 Dec. 1814, John McGuire sec.
Short, Clark & Margaret Mure 19 Dec. 1826, John Alverson sec.
Short, George & Frances Canadey 30 Dec. 1799, Samuel Johnston sec.
Short, George & Ellen Enniss 4 Nov. 1830, John W. Howsen sec.
Short, Jeremiah & Neely Hollinshead -- 1810, William Hall - Badly
    Damaged.
Short, John & Anne Owens, wid. 6 Oct. 1790, Brown Robinson sec.
Short, John & Maria Spurling 2 Jan. 1827, Elijah Williams sec.
Short, Landman & Susannah Tait 28 May 1793, William Bettisworth
    sec.
Short, Silas & Jane Sanders 11 Feb. 1817, James Fisher sec.
Short, Silas & Catherine Jett, 3 June 1821, Henry C. Bragg sec.
Short, Thomas & Mary Ann Brown, dau. Ann Owen, 23 Oct. 1789,
    Landman Short sec.
Short, Thomas & Peggy Gregory 2 Sept. 1796, James Gregory sec.
Short, William Walker & Ann Smith -- June 1789, William Kenner sec.
Short, William & Alcey Whitley 5 May 1818, Catesby C. Collinsworth
    sec.

Silba, John A. & Lucy Ann Lee 15 Jan. 1837, John Spillman sec.

Silby, John & Sally Fones - Not dated (Bundle marked "1803")
    Bond signed but not filled in - George Field sec.

Silvey, Abraham & Elizabeth Spilmore 16 Sept. 1806, James Brown
    sec.

Simms, Benjamin & Mary McDaniel 1 Jan. 1820, Thomas N. Berryman
    sec.
Simms, James & Nancy Johnson dau. Elizabeth Johnson, 14 Sept.
    1806, Richard H. Simms sec.

Sisson, Barrett & Frances Brown 9 June 1809, Will: Settle sec.
Sisson, George & Mary S. Redman 26 June 1797, Catesby Jones sec.
Sisson, George & Mary Mullins 15 Nov. 1820, John Spence sec.
Sisson, George H. & Susan P. Butler 25 Aug. 1845, Augustine
    Quisenbury sec.
Sisson, Martin & Caty Moxley 4 Nov. 1797, Edward Sanford sec.
    Badly Damaged.
Sisson, Redman & Elizabeth A. Webb 29 Dec. 1846, William Richards
    sec.
Sisson, William & Peggy Muse 16 Dec. 1789, Charles Muse sec.
Sisson, William H. & Susanna W. Sandford 19 Jan. 1824, John Sandy
    sec.
Sisson, William R. & Ann E. Harvey 24 May 1825, Joseph F. Harvey
    sec.
Sisson, William H. & Elizabeth Sandy 21 July 1834, John B. Sisson
    sec.

Skinner, George G. & Ann M. Frank 11 Dec. 1833, James E. Deatley
    sec.

Smaw, John & Jemima Crabb 12 Dec. 1786, Ashton Lamkin sec.

Smith, Baldwin B. & Elizabeth Jackson 20 Dec. 1796, J. A. Thompson
sec.
Smith, Emanuel & Juliet Ashton 7 Jan. 1830, James G. Donoho sec.
Smith, George Bailey & Ann Deatterly 6 May 1788, Christopher
Deatterly sec.
Smith, George & Martha Attwell 6 Dec. 1797, John Smith sec.
Smith, George & Betsey Batton 26 Sept. 1805, James Batton sec.
Smith, George William & Ann Campbell 5 Oct. 1820, Joseph Fox sec.
Smith, Jeremiah & Fenny Sutton 3 Feb. 1824, Vincent Sutton sec.
Smith, John W. & Meriah Thompson 13 Feb. 1804, William Thompson,
Jr. sec.
Smith, Dr. John Augustine & Letitia Lee 3 Apr. 1809, J.W.Jones
sec.
Smith, John T. & Mary M. Smith, dau. William W. Smith, 25 Dec.
1822, James S. Monroe sec.
Smith, John C. & Mary Jane Lamkin 12 Sept. 1844, James W.
English sec.
Smith, John G. of Richmond County, & E. V. Costin, 25 Apr. 1849,
Benedict P. Crabb sec.
Smith, Peter & Sarah Smith 28 Dec. 1789, William Brickey sec.
Smith, Peter, & Polly Pillman 26 Aug. 1823, Benedict Walker sec.
Smith, Philip P. & Sally B. Newton 26 Mar. 1849, Edward C.
Griffith sec.
Smith, Richard & Eliza Ann King 11 Jan. 1830, William Brann sec.
Smith, Samuel & Elizabeth Harrison 13 May 1791, Richard Smith
sec.
Smith, William W. & Betsey Monroe, dau. David Monroe, 9 July,
1793, Lee Pitman sec.
Smith, William B. & Nancy Butler 1 Apr. 1806, George Moore sec.

Smither, Hiram & Sally Carter 11 June 1824, William J. Courtney
sec.

Sorrell, John Wesley & Sarah Sanford 23 Dec. 1847, George H.
Bryan sec.
Sorrell, Spencer & Nancy Guttridge 21 Jan. 1831, Meredith Lucas
sec.
Sorrell, Spencer & Letta Marks 24 Dec. 1845, William L. Mothers-
head sec.
Sorrell, Thomas & Elizabeth Lucass, dau. John Lucass, 3 Dec.
1794, Lawrence Lucas sec.
Sorrell, Thomas A. & Nancy Attwell, dau. William Attwell, 18
Aug. 1807, James Johnson sec.

Spark, George & Polly Jones 26 Apr. 1834, William George Walker
sec.
Spark, James & Hannar Parker 10 July 1791, Richard Parker sec.

Sparks, George & Ann Sanford Hall 19 May 1825, Charles Teet sec.
Sparks, William & Lucy Redman 6 Jan. 1801, Charles Muse sec.

Spence, Edward & Sally Sisson 11 Dec. 1809, Charles Muse sec.
Spence, John & Mary A. Bragg, 4 Nov. 1837, William Burgess sec.

Spence, Thomas & Caty Sanford, alias Caty Pope, 15 Dec. 1788,
    James Rice sec.
Spence, Thomas & Mary C. Brown -- 1809. William Brown sec.
Spence, Thomas B. & Mary E. Lewis 20 Jan. 1842, Samuel B. Atwill
    sec.
Spence, William & Winny Sisson 10 June 1805, John Sisson sec.

Spilman, George S. & Frances Neale 16 Jan. 1823, Landon Carter
    sec.
Spilman, John & Thirza Hoult 3 May 1815, Abraham White sec.

Spriggs, Nathan & Elizabeth C. Brinnon 26 Aug. 1795, Lewis
    Chastain sec.

Spurling, Elisha & Elizabeth M. Cary 23 Jan. 1815, Vincent
    Edmonds sec.
Spurling, James & Charlotte Carpenter 3 Jan. 1792, James Jewell
    sec.
Spurling, Reubin & Molly Pumroy 13 Oct. 1801, William Hazzard
    sec.
Spurling, William & Nancy Cary 23 Mar 1799, George Carey sec.
Spurling, William & Ann Eliza Hazard 22 Mar. 1830, William
    Hazard sec.

Standley, William & Frances Walker - Consent of Frances Walker
    dated 10 Dec. 1803, Witnessed by Solomon Robinson -
    Bond signed but not filled in - Joel Rose sec.

Starr, Seth & Elizabeth Lawson Eskridge 7 Apr. 1789, John Esk-
    ridge sec.

Starke, Henry D. & Elizabeth McCarty 21 Mar. 1826, William
    Robinson sec.

Stewart, Benjamin F. & Mary Jett Harvey, day. Lucy Harvey, 20
    Nov. 1826, Daniel Carmichael sec.
Stewart, John & Ann Carmichael 8 Dec. 1789, John Butler sec.
Steward, John & Fanney Hore 21 Mar. 1810, Joseph Fox sec.
Stewart, Richard & Margaret McCarty 27 July 1802, Joseph Fox,Jr.
    sec.
Stewart, Thomas & Susan King 26 Dec. 1831, George King sec.

Steel, Benjamin & Ellen Deatterly 21 Jan. 1795, Christopher
    Deatterly sec.
Steel, John Brown & Sarah Collinsworth 31 Jan. 1788, John Collins-
    worth sec.
Steel, Richard & Susanna Monroe 9 Apr. 1801. George Field sec.
Steel, Thomas & Jemima Bartley 22 Sept. 1790, John Higdon sec.

Sterling, Samuel & Rebeckah Johnson 15 Nov. 1833, James Dunahaw
    sec.

Stephens, James & Nancy Douglas, dau. John Douglas - Consent of
John Douglas dated 20 Dec. 1801.
Stephens, James & Nancy Douglas 21 Dec. 1801, John D. Olive sec.
Stephens, James B. & Winneyfred King, dau. James King, 13 July,
1826, Jeremiah Stephens sec.
Stephens, James & Mary Carpenter 2 Apr. 1832, Joseph Moon sec.
Stephens, Jeremiah & Winifred Willson 28 July 1798, William P.
Cratb sec.
Stephens, Jeremiah & Hannah J. Cole 15 Mar. 1826, William Cole
sec.
Stephens, John B. & Alice Hall 11 Sept. 1837, Henry Stephens sec.
Stephens, Robert & Julion Hudson, dau. William R. Hudson, 14
Sept. 1847, James R. Courtney sec.

Stiff, Robert & Ann C. B. Broughton 13 Dec. 1831, John H. Peake
sec.

Stone, Edward & Jemima Sanford 7 Jan. 1796, Anthony A. Harrison
sec.
Stone, Elliott & Ann Clarke 9 Feb. 1818, Thomas Clarke sec.
Stone, Isaac & Nancy Jett 19 Oct. 1786, William Jett sec.
Stone, Joseph & Elizar Fairfax Stone, dau. Alice Stone, 3 Sept.
1827, Edward Stone sec.
Stone, Presly & Fanny Baker Blundell 25 Aug. 1796, Thomas Blun-
dell sec.
Stone, Thomas & Alice Bruer 2 Jan. 1788, Edward Sanford sec.
Stone, Thomas & Catherine Clark 25 May 1850, Thomas W. Clark sec.
Stone, William & Sarah Morris 25 Jan. 1791, Sanders Morris sec.
Stone, William & Peggy Morris, dau. Charles Morris, 9 Mar. 1793,
Youell Morris sec.
Stone, William J. & Eliza H. Clayton 24 Mar. 1815, William Y.
Sturman sec.
Stone, William B. & Martha Hall 12 Oct. 1821, William B. Hall sec.

Stoner, Peter of Cumberland County & Frances Minor, spinster, 7
Apr. 1772, Griffin Fauntleroy of Northumberland County sec.

Stowers, Thomas & Keziah Robinson 18 July 1793, John McClanahan
sec.
Stowers, Thomas & Sarah Butler - Consent of Sarah Butler dated
21 Dec. 1801

Straughn, James & Louisa F. Hawkins 29 Sept. 1825, Griffin R.
Kirk sec.
Straughan, Thomas N. & Sarah E. Oldham, dau. John F. Oldham,
18 Jan. 1847, Joseph A. Booth sec.

Sturman, Foxall & Elizabeth Neale 2 Dec. 1810, Willis Garner sec.

Suit, William & Elizabeth Abton 12 June 1846, Robert Anton sec.
Sutc, William & Zalea Monzer Mazerean 18 May 1850, Benjamin
Anton sec.

Sullivan, Owen & Nancy Beale 20 June 1816, George N. Cluskey sec.
Sullivan, Owen & Sally Booth 5 Apr. 1837, Edward T. Sanford sec.
Sullivan, Owen & Mary Hall 23 Feb. 1839, Rodham Douglass sec.

Sutton, Edward & Sally Anthony - Consent of Sally Anthony - In
Bundle marked "1807" - Witnessed by W. Butler - Bond
signed but not filled in - William Butler sec.
Sutton, George & Nancy Packett - Consent of Nancy Packett dated
1 Nov. 1811 - Witnessed by Jeremiah Sutton
Sutton, James & Frances White, wid. 3 Oct. 1786, Thomas Pritchett
sec.
Sutton, James & Molly Hawkins 21 Dec. 1804, James Dunnahau sec.
Sutton, James & Elizabeth Nelson 28 June 1816 -
Sutton, John S. & Rebecca Eskridge 29 Aug. 1791, Thomas H. Moore
sec.
Sutton, John & Martha Stone 31 Aug. 1819, Robert Hall sec.
Sutton, John W. & Sarah R. Robinson 29 June 1837, Vincent B.
McKenny sec.
Sutton, John & Ann Watson 24 June 1839, Edwin G. Reed sec.
Sutton, Josiah & Elizabeth Davis, dau. Elias Davis, 24 Nov. 1789
James Rowles sec.
Sutton, Joseph & Martha Crask 5 Mar. 1811, George Cavender sec.
Sutton, Reuben G. & Sarah Ann Mullins 20 Sept. 1794, Thomas H.
Moore sec.
Sutton, Richard & Fanny Chilton 6 Mar. 1839 William Sanford sec.
Sutton, Samuel & Elizabeth Crask 24 Dec. 1817, Joseph Sutton sec.
Sutton, Thomas & Nancy Robinson 28 Mar. 1789, Thomas Pritchett
sec.
Sutton, Tryan & Elizabeth R. Dozier 18 Jan. 1819, William R.
Dozier sec.
Sutton, William, Jr. & Trucy M. Sutton 9 Sept. 1817, M.C.Harvey
sec.
Sutton, William & Sarah Brinnon 11 Dec. 1832, Newman McKenney sec.
Sutton, William & Kitty Nash 6 Jan. 1835, William T. Brown &
William H. Sanford sec.
Sutton, William & Alice McKenney 20 Apr. 1836, Richard Donnahaw
sec.
Sutton, William R. & Susan R. Redman 15 Nov. 1849, William R.
Dozier sec.

Sydnor, Richard B. & Hannah C. Mothershead, dau. G. G. Mothershead, 19 Apr. 1847, James C. Harvey sec.

Taliaferro, Charles & Susanna Moxley 31 Jan. 1812, David T.
Chevis sec.
Taliaferro, John T. & E. Maria Parker 21 Oct. 1848, Robert S.
Bailey sec.

Tallant, Bethal & Nancy Henage 13 June 1816, William L. Mothers-
head soc.
Tallant, George F. & Elizabeth Hinson 1 Jan. 1817, William
Wallant sec.
Tallant, James & Elizabeth Rowe 30 Dec. 1845, Henry Rowe sec.

Tallent, Christopher & Lettice Garner 16 June 1823, Richard J.
Brown sec.
Tallent, Christopher & Catherine Short 2 Aug. 1826, John M.
Marmaduke sec.
Tallent, John L. & Amy Marks 31 Jan. 1828, Richard Onohundro sec.
Tallent, John L. & Mary A. Nash 4 May 1848, Alexander Carpenter
sec.
Tallent, William, Jr. & Lucy Davis 19 Feb. 1824, Samuel Davis sec.
Tallent, William, Jr. & Ann Jenkins 30 Oct. 1828, John M. Marma-
duke sec.
Tallent, William, Jr. & Amelia S. Yeatman 11 June 1834, John
Hunter sec.

Tapscott, John S. & Elizabeth Attwell 19 Jan. 1800, Daniel Crabb,
Jr. sec.
Tapscott, John S. & Sally Cain 7 July 1803, William Sisson sec.
Tapscott, Robert H. & Mary E. Wright 9 May 1822, Thomas M. Bragg
sec.

Taite, Joseph & Felicia Ashton 28 Dec. 1897, Lawrence Ashton sec.
Taite, Samuel & Elizabeth Marmaduke 11 July 1822, John Spence sec.

Tate, Anderson, & Juliann Lucas 9 Jan. 1845, Mark Lucas sec.
Tate, Berryman & Ann Thompson 30 Mar 1836, Simon Tate sec.
Tate, Campbell & Mary Ann Lucas 31 Dec. 1845, Mark Lucas sec.
Tate, Edmond & Peggy Aston 12 Dec. 1806, Joseph Tate sec.
Tate, Ephram & Clara Johnson 13 Mar. 1850, J. L. Davis sec.
Tate, Henry & Sintha Johnson 10 Jan. 1831, Campbell Tate sec.
Tate, Hopeful & Maria Tate 23 Jan. 1832, Samuel Tate sec.
Tate, James & Charity Grimes 22 Aug. 1804, Nathaniel Brewer sec.
Tate, Jordan & Betsy Thompson, dau. Bennett Thompson, 6 Oct.
1838, William B. Butler sec.
Tate, Lewis, & Hannah Sale 6 Apr. 1825, Reuben Muse sec.
Tate, Nathaniel & Hannah Johnson 28 Dec. 1843, John Ashton,Sr. sec.
Tate, Samuel & Hannar Lucas 30 Dec. 1809, Laurence Ashton sec.
Tate, Samuel & Eliza Newman 30 Apr. 1846, Hopeful Tate sec.
Tate, Simon & Lowery Tate 6 Jan. 1830, Bland Ashton sec.
Tate, William & ------ Pumroy ------ 1805 - Badly Damaged.
Tate, William & Elizabeth Hinson, dau. Ann Hinson, 20 Dec. 1847,
Samuel C. F. Butler sec.
Tate, Umphrey & Doxsey Ashton 19 Dec. 1838, Blain Ashton sec.

Taylor, David B. & Fanny P. Bailey 13 Dec. 1826, Robert Bailey sec.

Teet, Campbell Robinson & Peggy E. Cole 7 Mar. 1791, Nathaniel
Locust sec.
Teet, Campbell R. & Elizabeth Mothershead 12 Dec. 1796, Richard
B. Johnson sec.
Teet, Campbell, Jr., son of Charles Teet, & Elizabeth Pumroy, 3
Dec. 1819, James Deakins sec.
Teet, Charles & Betsey Barker 11 May 1825, Campbell Teet sec.
Teet, Lovell & Elizabeth Reamy 14 Dec. 1825, James Cooke sec.

Teet, Thomas & Mary Robinson - Consent of Mary Robinson dated 31
    Jan. 1799 - Witnessed by Elizabeth Adkins & Campbell R. Teet
    Bond signed but not filled in ------us Edmunds sec. Badly
    Damaged.
Tete, William B. & Sintha Tete, dau. James Tete, 27 Dec. 1824,
    Eason G. Jones sec.
Teet, William & Ann Nash -- Feb. 1835, James R. Atwell sec.
Teete, Youell & Grace Newman 26 Jan. 1821, Dennis Newman sec.

Templeman, John & Ellen Lawson 30 Apr. 1788, Richard Bruer sec.
Templeman, Samuel & Caty McKenny 4 Aug. 1807, Gerard McKenny sec.

Tennent, George Washington & Ann Campbell, dau. Susanna Campbell,
    -- Nov. 1803, Joseph Fox, Jr. sec.

Terrell, John W. & Eliza James 5 Nov. 1832, George G. Barak sec.

Thomas, Becham & Nelly Anthony 5 July 1813, Thomas Spence sec.
Thomas, James & Darky Thomas 22 June 1807, George Weldon sec.
Thomas, William P. & Elizabeth Barrot 2 May 1825, William W.
    Owens sec.
Thomas, William & Margaret Mure 21 June 1826, John Crenshaw sec.
Thomas, William & Mary Williams 4 May 1831, Jeremiah Courtney sec.

Thompson, Benjamin & Mary Thompson 5 Jan. 1847, Henry S. Johnson
    sec.
Thompson, Burnett & Barbara Bell 18 Dec. 1807, William Thornton
    Peirce sec.
Thompson, Charles R. & Mary Jackson, dau. Rebecca Jackson, 25
    Jan. 1792, William P. Quarles sec.
Thompson, George, son of James Thompson,& Easter Harrison 3 Jan.
    1849, Solomon Dixon sec.
Thomson, Henry & Catherine McGuy 29 Sept. 1789, Bennett McGuy sec.
Thompson, James A. & Rebecca Newton Jackson, dau. Rebecca
    Jackson, 30 Jan. 1790, Willoughby Newton sec.
Thompson, Jarrat & Betsy McKoy 21 May 1822
Thompson, John & Sarah A. Asden, dau. Winny Asden 11 Mar. 1830,
    Alec Thompson sec.
Thompson, Joseph, Gentleman, & Judith B. Rowand, born 25 Mar.
    1773 -"From a book containing the private Register-
    Thomas Rowand the father, Mary Kenner the mother,
    Thomas & John Rowand the brothers to the above mentioned
    Judith B. Rowand" 12 May 1794, Martin Tapscott sec.
Thompson, Moses & Henrietta Thompson, dau. Bennitt Thompson,
    7 Jan. 1845, Solomon Dixon sec.
Thompson, Richard & Jane Nelson 23 Mar. 1798, John Porter sec.
Thompson, Richard & Sally Yeatman, dau. Thomas Yeatman, 25 June
    1798, Edward Sanford sec.

Thorpe, Thomas & Elizabeth Butler, dau. Christopher Butler, 10
    Sept. 1795, William Butler sec.

Thrift, Jeremiah & Elizabeth Self 25 Jan. 1810, Francis Self sec.
Thrift, Jeremiah C. & Alice J.Gawin 7 Dec. 1847, William H.Self
    sec.

Thrift, Joseph B. & Mary Ann Branson 11 Apr. 1848, Thomas H.
Bragg, sec.
Thrift, Samuel & Ann Self 29 Aug. 1795, William Hail sec.
Thrift, Samuel R. & Eliza A. Tinsley dau. Cinthia Tinsley, 19
Dec. 1838, Richard H. Donnahaw sec.

Ticer, William & Ann Butler 30 July 1828, Enoch G. Jeffries sec.

Tiffy, Pope & Elizabeth Vigar 24 Aug. 1801, Lawrence Pope sec.
Tiffey, Richard V. & Ann Nelson 22 June 1829, William Butler sec.

Tippit, John & Mary Clark 27 Sept. 1791, John Brawner sec.

Toombs, Dawson G. & Mary Kelsick 8 Dec. 1797, Benjamin Dawson sec.

Travers, Capt. Devereaux B. & Rebeccah R. Garner 1 Nov. 1826,
Robert Bailey sec.

Triplett, Francis C. & Sarah Mariner 9 Feb. 1810, Richard N.
Mariner sec.
Triplett, William H. & Eliza M. Richardson -- Dec. 1828, William
G. Walker sec.

Trigger, Francis & Ann Drake 20 June 1787, Robert Steel sec.

True, James & Sarah E. Pitts, dau. Patsy Pitts, 16 June 1845,
William True sec.
True, William & Elizabeth Weldon, dau. George Weldon, 29 Dec.
1808, George Weldon sec.
True, William & Eliza J. Spilman 28 Feb. 1838, James Mariner sec.

Tupman, John & Patsey Thomas 26 July 1787, Meredith Thomas sec.

Turnbull, George & Sally Spence 6 Sept. 1787, Thomas Muse sec.

Turberville, John & Ann Ballantine, wid. 19 Dec. 1792, James
Bland sec.
Turberville, Richard Lee & Henrietta Lee, dau. Ann Lee, 13 Dec.
1794, George Thomson sec.

Turner, Charles B. of Northumberland, & Judith B. Parker 8 Dec.
1838, David H. Tapscott sec.
Turner, Henry & Mary Chambers 30 Jan. 1850, Thomas Chambers sec.
Turner, John & Susanna Butler 17 Apr. 1795, James Butler sec.
Turner, William & Nancy Conkling, wid. 28 Jan. 1794, John Monroe
sec.

Tuxan, Charles F. N. (free negro) & Polly Carter 6 Jan. 1819,
Dennis Newman sec.

Underwood, John & Molly Muse 19 Mar. 1792, Walker Muse sec.
Underwood, John & Frances Washington 27 Jan. 1813, John Randall
    sec.

Vaughan, James & Ann Tiffey 10 Feb. 1834, John Roane sec.

Waller, Edward & Sally Callis 31 Jan. 1787, Samuel Bailey sec.

Wallace, Aaron & Elizabeth Brann 21 Dec. 1818, John Redman sec.
Wallace, Capt. Aaron & Frances Redman 31 Jan. 1825, William
    Coghill sec.
Wallace, William & Mary Jane Jett, dau. Charles Jett, 17 Nov.
    1849, Henry T. Jett sec.

Walker, Benedict & Charlotte Smith - Consent of Charlotte Smith
    dated 1 Jan. 1809, Witnessed by Sally B. Smith - Bond
    signed but not filled in - Dozier Lyell sec.
Walker, Benedict & Hannah Wright 19 Jan. 1825, James C. Wright
    sec.
Walker, George & Sally Robinson, dau. Joseph Robinson of North-
    umberland, 27 Feb. 1812, Daniel Harrison sec.
Walker, Richard & Mary P. Morgan 22 May 1797, William King sec.
Walker, Samuel & Ann Montgomery 23 Jan. 1797, James Montgomery sec.
Walker, William & Elizabeth Hughs 22 Sept. 1798, Thomas Hughs sec.
Walker, William & Elizabeth S. Packett 12 Jan. 1806, William M.
    Walker sec.
Walker, William M. & Sebella P. Field 22 July, 1807, Richard T.
    Brown sec.
Walker, William G. & Elizabeth Sanford 17 Apr. 1844, Joseph S.
    Lyell sec.

Wardrobe, David & Elen Garner 30 Dec. 1789, James Bland sec.
Wardrobe, David, Polly Mezick 17 May 1811, John W. Jones sec.

Waring, Eppephroditus Lawson & Elizabeth Bankhead, 30 Oct. 1817,
    Robert G. Robb sec.
Warring, Henry & Lucy Robb 30 Apr. 1821, Joseph Fox sec.

Washington, Corbin & Hannah Lee 8 May 1787, James Bland sec.
Washington, Henry & Jane Winkfield 6 Jan. 1845, Walker Winkfield
    sec.
Washington, John & Lucy Hinson 10 June 1816, William Nash sec.
Washington, John & Jane Davis 20 Dec. 1837, Joseph L. Lyle sec.
Washington, Lawrence & Sarah F. Washington 25 Oct. 1819 J. H.
    Jett sec.
Washington, Lawrence & Sarah F. Washington, married in West-
    moreland County 26 Oct. 1819, by William H. Wilmer,
    Rector of St. Pauls Church, Alexandria, - Certificate
    of Rev. William H. Wilmer.

Washington, Thomas & Sarah Harper , wid. 16 May 1788, Henry
Washington sec.
Washington, Thomas & Patsey Teet, 23 Dec. 1816, James Hinson sec.

Watson, George & Hannah Brawner 18 Aug. 1815 Thomas Mothershead
sec.
Watson, William & Caty Collins 2 Dec. 1800, James Briant sec.

Watkins, Thomas G. & Susan Jackson, dau. Samuel Jackson, 10 Oct.
1802, H. Jackson sec.

Waters, Joseph B. & Matilda Airs 27 Mar. 1826, Robert H. Tapscott
sec.
Waters, Joseph B. & Ann C. Wann daughter Walter Wann, 4 June
1831, William Jackson sec.

Watts, Caleb & Margaret Lauder, dau. James Lauder 20 Jan. 1818,
George B. Smith sec.

Waughan, Walter & Polly McKy dau. James & Mary McKy 22 Sept
1807, Samuel Gilbert sec.

Weaver, Alexander & Harriott Annadale 7 Jan. 1809, David
Annadale sec.
Weaver, Alexander & Marthy Alderson 3 July 1821, James Mariner
sec.
Weaver, Alfred & Mary Clark 14 May 1821, Richard Clark sec.
Weaver, Benjamin & Alice Weaver 20 Dec. 1819, Robert G. Robb
sec.
Weaver, Elijah & Elizabeth Frary (contemporary records in-
dicate "Tracy") 8 Apr. 1796, Richard Clayton sec.
Weaver, Frederick & Kitty Reamey, dau. James Reamey, 4 Jan.
1848, Martin Killmon sec.
Weaver, Henry & Ann Omohundro, 18 Feb. 1824
Weaver, Henry & Ann Edmonds, dau. Mary Edmonds -- 183(8) James
B. Balderson sec.
Weaver, Henry & Catherine C-------- 15 June, 1842, George G.
Mothershead sec.
Weaver, Henry & Jane Nash 1 Dec. 1847, William Nash sec.
Weaver, James & Ailsey Sutton. Consent of Ailsey Sutton dated
22 Dec. 1808 - Bond signed but not filled in.
Reuben Sutton sec.
Weaver, James A. & Jane P. Rose 24 Nov. 1845, Conaway Reynolds
sec.
Weaver, John & Mary Williams 7 June 1791, John Marmaduke sec.
Weaver, John & Penny Sanford 24 Mar. 1792, William Omohundro sec.
Weaver, John & Labiey Bryant 27 Apr. 1806, Levy Bryant sec.
Weaver, John, son of henry, & Emily M. Bragg 23 Nov. 1849,
Robert M. Bragg sec.
Weaver, Presley & Mary Alverson 21 Jan. 1824, Joshua Reamy sec.
Weaver, Richard & Elizabeth Carter 30 Aug. 1806

Weaver, Richard & Ann Jenkins 1 Dec. 1819, James Brown sec.
Weaver, Samuel & Martha Gregory 7 Oct. 1816, Alexander Weaver sec.
Weaver, Sidnall & Elizabeth Harris 12 Feb. 1821, Levi Briant sec.
Weaver, Thomas & Mary Annandale 11 June 1806, Barnet Goode sec.
Weaver, William & Elizabeth Collins 4 Dec. 1798, Tapley Brand -
     Badly Damaged
Weaver, William & Ann Davis 9 June 1834, Samuel Davis sec.

Weatherespoon, William & Joyce Butler 25 May 1790, Charles Weeks
     sec.

Webb, Beverly S. & Mary S. Harper 31 Dec. 1847, William Richards
     sec.
Webb, William & Frances F. Rose, 3 Sept. 1846, William G. Sturman
     sec.

Weeks, Benjamin Pope & Mary Smith - Consent of Lusitta Smith,
     guardian of Mary Smith dated 23 Nov. 1796 - Bond dated
     28 Nov. 1796, Thomas N. Buryman sec.

Weedon, John T. & Ann M. VanNess, dau. of B. VanNess, 25 July
     1836, John M. Carpenter sec.

Weldon, George H. & Mary Gaskins 29 Jan. 1828, Samuel Harrison
     sec.

Werrell, Austin & Jane Pursley 24 Apr. 1832, James Eidson sec.

Wheatley, Thomas & Alcy Collinsworth, dau. William Collinsworth,
     28 July, 1812, John Hunter sec.
Wheatley, William & Sally Brinnon 26 July, 1813, John B. Steel
     sec.

Wheeler, Frederick & Maria L. Collins 29 May 1841, D. H.
     Tapscott sec.
Wheeler, Capt. William & Eliza Brinnan 3 Jan. 1838, Joseph Moon
     sec.

Whittington, Thomas & Frances Nelms Turner, dau. Susanna Hall,
     11 May 1810, John Tapscott & Philip White sec.

White, Benjamin & Mary Quisenbury - Consent of William Quisenbury
     dated 26 Apr. 1813, Witnessed by William C. Quisenbury,
     Jr.
White, Gowan R. & Mary F. Beale 24 Jan. 1842, Thomas T. Beale sec.
White, Granville & Leannah Mothershead, dau. Sarah Mothershead,
     3 Mar. 1838, James True sec.
White, John & Elisha Mothershead 25 Mar. 1799, Nathaniel Mothers-
     head sec.
White, William & Sarah Kitchen 1 Jan. 1787, James Bland sec.
White, William & Ann Dishman 1 Mar. 1810, William Dishman sec.
White, William & Susan Dishman 14 Mar. 1836, Samuel Dishman sec.

Wickliff, Charles & Susannah Nelson 10 Feb. 1789, Vincent
Saunders sec.

Wigley, James & Jane Clark, wid., 23 Sept. 1786, James Briant sec.
Wigley, James & Elizabeth Barrott 10 Dec. 1804, John Brawner sec.

Wills, George & Prudence Bowden 4 Jan. 1791, Jesse Fowler sec.

Williams, Elijah & Juliana McKildoe 16 Sept. 1826, John B. Curtis
sec.
Williams, Levin & Bridget Beacham 27 Aug. 1838, Thomas Parks sec.
Williams, Thomas & Sarah Hodge 19 Oct. 1789, Willoughby Harrison
sec.
Williams, Thomas & Jane Garner 23 Dec. 1805, Presley Garner sec.
Williams, William & Alice Carnaday 4 Jan. 1796 John Butler sec.
Williams, William & Margaret T. Branson, dau. Newyear Branson,
14 Jan. 1805, Matthew J. Courtney sec.
Williams, William, son of Peter Williams & Fanny Dean, dau. John
Dean, 7 Aug. 1824, William Lawrence sec.

Wilson, Daniel, of Richmond County, & Rebecah Bartlett, 20 Oct.
1806, Jeremiah Jones sec.
Willson, Edward & Lucy Fones 5 May 1804, James Scales sec.
Wilson, George & Sarah Bartlett, 15 Dec. 1826, Joel Bartlett sec.
Wilson, George & Ann King, dau. Mary King, 25 Oct. 1839, Edwin G.
Reed sec.
Wilson, Henry & Lucy Ann Eliff 10 Aug. 1838, John Fones sec.
Wilson, James & Sally Hughsencraft 25 Nov. 1802, George Connolly
sec.
Wilson, James & Susan Bowen 16 June 1828, Thomas Moss sec.
Wilson, Robert & Frances Bennett 10 Jan. 1850, James Johnson sec.
Willson, William & Elizabeth Hinson - Consent of Elizabeth Hinson
dated 7 Apr. 1802, Witnessed by Daniel Willson & Samuel
Ryals - Bond signed but not filled in - Badly Damaged-
sec. gone.
Willson, William & Sally Willson, wid. 30 May 1815, John Jenkins
sec.
Wilson, William H. & Ann M. F. Cox 6 July, 1835, Darius G. Cralle
sec.

Wilkins, George & Mary G. Hail 22 Apr. 1816, Richard Knott sec.
Wilkins, John & Eliza A. King, dau. James King, 19 June, 1843,
Richard R. King sec.
Wilkins, Mathew & Lucretia Atkins, dau. Jane Atkins, 15 July 1843
Joseph Atkins sec.
Wilkins, Richard & Susanna Deatly 25 Aug. 1806, John Nash sec.
Wilkins, Richard & Jane Mitchell 24 Oct. 1814, James Bartlett sec.
Wilkins, Robert E. & Sally S. Bozman 3 Sept. 1830, Robert Scott
sec.

Wilkerson, Austin & Susanna Brennon 29 Jan. 1823, Austin B. Frank
sec.
Wilkerson, ---- & Anne Brinnon - Consent of Thomas Stowers dated
13 Jan. 1820

Wilkerson, Thomas & Sally Nelson 7 Aug. 1799, Barnett Wilerson
sec.

Winkfield, Henry & Sillar Lucas 4 Jan. 1826, Meredith Lucas sec.
Winkfield, Henry & Martha A. Marks 6 Jan. 1846, Henry Winkfield,
Sr. sec.
Winkfield, James & Winney Hammans 5 Oct. 1814, William Marks sec.
Winkfield, Richard & Mary Lawrence 18 July 1787, Thomas Taite
sec.

Wingfield, Walker & Mahala Lucust 6 June 1825 James Brown sec.

Worth, Spencer & Nancy Curtis 9 Dec. 1806, Thomas Gutridge sec.

Wood, John & Ann Price, wid. 27 May 1789, Martin Fisher sec.
Wood, John & Molly Cahall 22 Aug. 1787, Samuel Wood sec.

Woosoncroft, George & Sally Jenkins 11 June 1799, Joshua Sanford
sec.
Woosencroft, George & Mary Self 6 Nov. 1797, James Woosencroft
sec.

Woollard, John & Jemima Redman 29 Apr. 1788, Thomas Hinds sec.

Wormley, Isaac & Betsy Peirce 26 Dec. 1842 John Wormley sec.

Worth, Thomas & Nelly Drake 26 Feb. 1788 Franklin Simms sec.

Wright, Benedict & Mary Rust, dau. Vincent Rust, 20 Jan. 1792
John Rust sec.
Wright, Benedict & Hannah Claughton 23 Dec. 1807, George M.
Wright sec.
Wright, Benedict D. & Sally Smith 3 Apr. 1820, William Brann sec.
Wright, Edward Rodgers & Aggay Randall 9 Apr. 1787, Andrew
Brann sec.
Wright, Edward & Sally Silby 11 June 1810, Daniel Carter sec.
Wright, Johnson & Polly Dawson, dau. W. Dawson, 26 June 1792,
Richard Bennett sec.

Winget, Joseph & Maria Mothershead, 5 Oct. 1819, George Mothershead sec.

(Wright, Richard & Polly Attwell, dau. William Attwell, 25 Apr.
1812, William Middleton sec.)

Wroe, John & Mary Bryant, 26 Sept. 1820, Elliott Stone sec.
Wroe, John & Eliza B. Hudson 11 Oct. 1826, James King sec.
Wroe (Rowe), John & Helen H. Haynie, dau. Prestley Haynie 24
Dec. 1833, William Ticer sec.
Wroe, Samuel & Molley King 25 June 1801, John King sec.

Wroe, Samuel & Castella Nash 22 Dec. 1834, William Hennage sec.
Wroe, Samuel C. & Mane R. Harrison 13 May 1848, John English sec.
Wroe, William & Sarah Carter 27 June 1797, Daniel Barkett sec.
Wroe, William & Dorotha Sandy, dau. Joanna Sandy, 23 Dec. 1848,
      Henry D. Barber sec.

Wrone, John & Lucy L. Ware dau. Walter Ware, 15 Jan. 1838, James
      Ware sec.

Yardley, James & Joyce Lucas, dau. Meredith Lucas, 31 July, 1815,
      James Edmonds sec.
Yardley, William & Nancy Pumroy, 17 Dec. 1810, William Tate sec.
Yardley, William & Lucy Oliff, 27 Jan. 1834, James Yardley sec.

Yeatman, Alfred J. & Emily Jane Hunter 2 Dec. 1834, William P.
      Crabb sec.
Yeatman, Henry L. & Alice Monroe 8 Aug. 1808, Thomas Brown sec.
Yeatman, Henry A., Sonn of Ann H. Yeatman, & Mary S. Crabb, dau.
      Jane Crabb, 14 Dec. 1827, G. G. Mothershead sec.
Yeatman, Jennings A. & Caty Sanford 25 June 1823, Benjamin
      Johnson sec.
Yeatman, Jesse & Jenny Brown 10 May 1791, Bryant Bailey sec.
Yeatman, John H. & Mary Burgess 10 Feb. 1809, James Burgess sec.
Yeatman, John B. & Catherine A. R. J. Maith 23 Apr. 1821,
      Samuel Smith sec.
Yeatman, Joseph & Mary Ann Dameron 1 June 1849, William A.
      Spence sec.
Yeatman, Joseph J. & Alice R. McKenney, 27 Dec. 1849, Presley
      McKenney sec.
Yeatman , Matthew & Eleanor Garner 1 Jan. 1811, Thomas Yeatman
      sec.
Yeatman, Robert & Mary Matthews, 14 Feb. 1839, R. W. Yeatman sec.
Yeatman, Robert W. & Martha Lucinda King, 19 Jan. 1844 -
      James C. Jackson, Joseph S. Lyell & H. H. Hazard sec.
Yeatman, Thomas & Elizabeth McClanahan 21 Jan. 1795, Edward
      Porter sec.
Yeatman, Thomas J. & Susan P. Hunter 11 Dec. 1839, Benett P.
      Crabb sec.

Young, Alexander & Nancy Green 26 Feb. 1788, William Gibson sec.

Acred, Betsy L. 15

Adams, Lucy 37

Adkins, Elizabeth 39

Airs, Matilda 74

Alderson, Marthy 74

Allison, Cloey 53

Alton, Lucinda 19

Alverson, Frances 38; Mary
74; Minty 5; Nancy
65; Sally 50

Ambrose, Nancy 64

Anderson, Ann M. 8;Elender
37; Elizabeth 8

Angel, Nancy 24

Anidd, Mary 30

Annodale, Cynthia 54

Annandale, Fanny 46; Harriott
74; Mary 75; Penny 54;

Anthoney, Kitty 7

Anthony, Nelly 71; Sally 59

Anton, Elizabeth 68; Mariah
9; Rebecca 36; Sarah 64

Arnest, Sophia T. 20

Arnol, Mary 49

Arnold, Julia (Alias Lovell)
25

Asden, Sarah A. 71

Ashton, Betsey 3; Doxey 70;
Felicia 70; Jane 39; Juliet
66; Lotty 18; Zenoba 3

Askins, Caty 24; Jane E. 48

Mary 41; Mary Ann 7; P. C. 25

Aston, Hannah B. 42; Peggy 70

Astin, Attoway 37; Patsy 13

Asting, Sarah Ann 30

Atkins, Elizabeth Ann 27;
Lucretia 76

Attwell, Elizabeth 70; Martha
45, 66; Nancy 66; Patty Rust
59; Polly 77; Sally 45;
Sarah D. 41

Atwill, Lucy B. 54

B

Baber, Amanda C. 55; Hannah C.
47; Jane 1

Bain, Nancy 63

Bailey, Frances 33; Frances A.
48; Frances L. 23; Fanny 16;
Fanny P. 70; Milly 50; Susan
62;

Baley, Winnaan 1

Baker, Susanha 23

Ball, Sarah 9

Balderson, Elizabeth 14; Frances
21; Nancey 6

Ballantine, Anne 48; 72; Elizabeth 23

Bankhead, Eliza 73; Eve 59

Barnes, Mary Ann 30; Nancy G. 53

Barber, Agnes 60; Charlott E. 21

Barker, Ann 61; Betsey 70; Eliza
40; Katharine 56; Margaret
34

Barrett, Ruthey 48

Barrot, Elizabeth 71

Barrott, Ann 15; Catharine 34; Elizabeth 76; Sally 56; Sarah 10

Barock, Ann A. 61

Barrack, Liza J. 56

Barnet, Nancy 26

Barnett, Alice 7; Eliza 11; Mary 22; Sally 49

Bartlet, Maria 64; Peggy Jett 50

Bartlett, Calista E. 41; Frances 34; Maria 23; Peggy 50; Penelope 37, 49; Rebecah 76; Sarah M. 41; Sarah 76; Susanna 63

Bartley, Jemima 67

Barecroft, Elizabeth 10; Winny 44

Brasshaw, Mary 10

Batten, Elizabeth 33

Batton, Betsey 66

Bayne, Martha 10; Leannah 62

Beane, Eleanor 44; Mary 23

Beann, Mary 4

Beale, Ann 6, 13, 38, 45; Elizabeth 10, 22; Elizabeth H. 18; Emily M. 2; Felicia 15; Hannah 46; Isabella 61; ; Martha F. 18 Mary 24; Mary F. 75; Mary J. 62; Nancy 69; Sally 2; Temperance 3;

Beacham, Ann G. 46; Bridget 76

Beddo, Fanny 47

Beddus, Nancy 38

Bell, Barbara 71

Benson, Nancy 10

Bennett, Mary 11,60; Frances 76

Berryman, Catherine 6

Berkley, Ann 6; Catherine B. 11; Elizabeth 19; Margaret N. 18; Mary Ann 53; Peggy 35; Susan A. 49

Betts, Caroline 11

Bettisworth, Nancy 36; Sally 25

Biggs, Elizabeth S. 39

Billins, Rebecca 2

Billings, Molley 26; Sally 18; Sarah 24

Biston, Nancy 48

Bispham,, Ann 43

Blackwell, Ann 10

Bland, Susanna 12

Blundell, Ann 30; Betsy 43; Fanny 17; Fanny Baker 68; Nancy B. 52

Bolderson, Jane 31

Booth, Sally 69

Boothe, Lydia 61

Boughton, Ann C.B. 68

Bowie, Rebecca 13; Sally Skinner 9

Bowen, Hany 55; Susan 76

Bowden, Nancy 3; Prudence 76

Bowcock, Catherine E. 39; Lucy P. 12

Boyer, Hannah 14

Boyd, Sarah 36

Bozman, Sally S. 76

Brawner, Ann 47; Frances 10;
Hannah 74; Mary 48

Brann, Alethea 61; Elizabeth
73; Lucy S. 64; Martha 12;
Nancy 24

Branham, Fanny 48

Branson, Cynthia 1; Mary Turner
36; Elizabeth A. 15; Mary
Ann 72; Margaret T. 76

Bragg, Eliza M. 42; Elizabeth
16; Emily M. 74; Martha 54;
Mary 63; Mary A. 66; Nancy
10; Ruth 48

Brewer, Catherine 12; Elizabeth
24,50; Haney 35; Lucy 57;
Sary 11

Brennon, Elizabeth 60; Rosannah
30; Susanna 76

Brinn, Elizabeth 38,41; Margaret
22

Brinon, Sarah 52

Brinnon, Anne 76; Eliza 75; Elizabeth C. 67; Fanny 8; Hannah
5; Sally 75; Sarah 69

Brinham, Alice 1

Briscoe, Elizabeth 4,38; Ellen 19,
55; Susannah 12

Briant, Fanny 37; Frankey 37

Brickley, Sally 51

Brickey, Nancy 60; Winney 58

Brockenbrough, Elizabeth 22

Brown, Ann C. 37; Catherine 10;
Charlotte 13; Elizabeth 9,29,
39; Fanny 9; Frances 62,65;

Jane 7; Jane A. 3; Jenny 78;
Maria 10; Martha 23; Marg-
aret 58; Margaret E.G. 38;
Mary 16; Mary Ann 65; Mary
C. 67; Mary J. 43; Nancy
64; Polly 34; Rebecca F. 10;
Rebecca 35,49; Sarah 52;
Sarah Ann 26

Bruce, Amelia 12, Caty 28; Cordelia 53; Harriott 53;
Sarah 11

Bruer, Alice 68

Bryant, Ann 38; Elizabeth 19;
Elizabeth S. 31; Mary 77;
Mary Ann 39; Sabrey 74

Buckley, Lucy 50; Sally 9

Bulger, Frances 34

Bunyan, Elizabeth 18; Nancy 51

Burn, Elizabeth 35; Mary E. 31

Burr, Ann 7

Burch, Eliza 13

Burkley, Mary 7

Burges , Mary 63

Burgess, Elizabeth 22,49; Keziah
1; Mary 78; Susannah 46

Burrell, Susanna 10

Burruss, Nancy 36

Butler, Alice 11; Ann 72; Elizabeth 20,25,71; Hannah
62; Jane Eliza 30; Joyce
75; Lucinda 1; Maria P. 54
Mary Hays 31; Nancy 66;
Polly 55; Sally 46; Sally E.
5; Sally M 30; Sarah 68;
Susan P. 55; Susanna 72

Coleman, Sarah 7

Collins, Caty 17,74; Elizabeth
75; Maria L. 75; Molley 41

Collinsworth, Alcy 75; Ann 24;
Fanny 14; Sarah 67; Sebinah
60

Combs, Jane Ellen 56

Conkling, Nancy 72

Connellee, Elizabeth A. 60;
Elizabeth T. 42

Cook, Alice 21; Christine 6;
Molley 21

Cooper, Ann 52; Sarah 13

Corbin, Eliza 3; Felicia 13;
. .. .9

Costin, Eleanor A. 9; E. V. 66

Courtney, Eliza 22; Elizabeth J.
29; Lydia A. 16; Mary W. 44
Peggy 60

Coward, Juliann 41

Cox, Ann M. 7; Ann M. F. 76;
Betsey 20; Eliza M. 49; Elizabeth R. 3; Mary E. 26,50.62;
Mary Susan 29; Roberta Ann 3;
Sally 59; Sarah 53; Sarah A.
7 Sarah Rickardia 59; Sarah S.
9

Crabb, Clarissa L. R. 21; Frances
46; Hannah G 3; Jane 3; Jane
Middleton 43; Jemima 65; Magdaline 24; Mary J. J. 65; Mary S.
78; Sally R. 12

Crask, Alcy 5; Ann 64; Ann H. 36;
Catherine 47; Elizabeth 27,51,
69; Frances T. 11; Martha 69;
Mary L. 57; Nancy 60; Sally 64

Cracy, Sally 64

Crenshaw, Elizabeth 8; Nancy 16;
Sally A. 59; Susanna 7

Critcher, Susanna 14,48

Cullison, Margaret 35

Curtis, Elizabeth 31,51; Franky
33; Hannah 4; Nancy 11,77;
Saly 18

Curtice, Haney 43; Rebecah 45

Curk, Jane 8

D

Daffaul, Polly 43

Dameron, Mahala Ann 30; Mary
38; Mary Ann 78

Darnaby, Margaret N. 44

Davis, Ann 75; Caty 49; Eliza
18; Elizabeth 36,59,69;
Fanny 24; Jane 73; Juliet
M. 21; Lucy 70; Lucinda 3;
Mary 10; Mary E. 67; Marg-
aret 18; Nancy 38; Nancy
Wright 37; Susan 13; Susan-
nah 45; Winney 41

Dawson, Polly 77

Day, Elizabeth 49; Judith 42

Deatley,---- 46; Alice 57; Anne
61; Ann Maria 5; Fanney 34;
Frances 5; Jane E, 57;
Lucinda 20,33; Mary M. 27;
Mary E. 2; Sara 64, Susanna
76

Deaterly, Ann 66; Ellen 67

Dean, Fanny 76; Mary Ann 53

Deane, Ann 36; Margaret 26;
Molly 31

Deen, Martha 27

Dekins, Elizabeth 40; Maria 15

Delano, Sarah Ann 22

Dement. Margaret L. 24

Dickie, Margaret 52

Dickerson, Nancy 54

Dirhman, Ann 75; Milly 37;
Nancy 58; Nancy T. 43; Susan
75; Susan R. 40

Dobbins, Elizabeth N. 37

Dodd, Ann 15; Delily 41; Elizabeth 2,27; Mary 23; Sophia
46

Dolman, Betsy 18; Ellin 62
Molley 32
Doleman, Elizabeth 3,21; Frances
B. 17; Nancy 17; Sarah 17

Donnahaw, Martha T. 32

Doulman, Caty 1

Douglas, Ann E. 50; Elizabeth 2
Nancy 68
Douglass, Agnes 42; Emily H. 21;
Mary W. 41; Molly 17

Downman, Elizabeth Ball 60

Downing, Elizabeth 52

Dozier, Amelia 42; Elizabeth 20,
34,47; Elizabeth R. 69;
Lucy 26; Mary 7; Mary E. 16;
Nancy S. 57

Drake, Ann 51,54,72; Catherine
28; Caty 53; Fanny 63; Nelly
77; Rachell 7; Saily 18;
Susan 27; Susannah 63

Dunton, Susanna 26

Dunbar, Elizabeth 60

Dunnahew, Ellin 49

Dye, Muriel V. 35

E

Eckles, Hannah 41

Edmons, Delilan 56; Nancy 21

Edmonds, Ann 74; Ann Jarvis 29;
Caty 4; Jane 36; Louisa 47

Lucy 26; Martha C. 15;
Sarah 15
Edmunds, Catherine 19

Edwards, Eliza 5; Elizabeth 26;
Frances 55; Jane Wilda 2;
Lucy Jane 22; Susan 32

Eidson, Elizabeth D. 34; Nancy
46; Susan 56

Eliff, Lucy Ann 76; Margaret E.
26

Elmore, Ann 5; Betsy 6; Catherine J. 6; Elizabeth 40,
48; Fanney 24; Harriet 6;
Jane 8,12; Maria 64; Mary
63; Susan 52

English, Ann H. 37; Elizabeth
B. 38; Jane Ann 6

Ennis, Haney 24; Libby 10

Enniss, Ellen 65

Eskridge, Elizabeth 10; Elizabeth Lawson 67; Rebecca
69; Venna 9

Eyles, Winefred 22

F

Fawbush, Lucy 55

Fegitt, Elizabeth 19

Fegget, Mariah 7

Figget, Matilda 47

Field, Mary Elizabeth 18;
Sebella P. 73

Fisher, Elizabeth 37; Felicia
63; Nancy 37; Peggy 1

Fitzgerald, Ann 26

Fitzhugh, Fanny 23

Fones. Delila P. 14; Flender 20;
Lucy R. 40; Lucy 76; Nancy 11;
Sally 65; Susan C. 57

Forbes, Louisa C. 52

Fox, Jenny 54; Lucette 29; Susannah 62

Foxhall, Nancy 9

France, Mary 20

Franklir, Ann 36; Feisin F. 4;
Mary 36

Frary, Elizabeth 74 (see Tracy)

Frank, Ann M. 65

Frame, Nancy 63

Fryer, Sarcus 49; Nancy 12

Fulcher, Sarah 50

G

Gallagher, Ann 12

Garner, Alice Jefferson 25;
Betsy 24; Caty 7,16; Darcus
5; Deborah 64; Elen 73; Eliza
62; Elizabeth 26; Eleanor 78;
Frances G. 6; Frances 10;
Jane 76; Lettice 17,25,78;
Lottey 54; Lydia E. B. 24;
Mary 33; Matilda 14; Nancy 6,
15; Peggy 33; Polly 17;
Rebeccah R. 72; Sarah 46;
Susan R. 64; Susanna 8; Winn-
ifred 12

Gardner, Tabitha 49

Garlick, Frances 8

Gaskins, Ann 12; Harriet 57;
Judy 12; Mary 75; Sarah 25

Gawn, Mary 46

Gawen, Lettis 20

Gawin; Alice J. 71; Catherine G. 46

Gill, Ann 16; Elizabeth 12

Gilbert, Frances M. 44; Nancy
17

Goldman, Ann 34

Good, Ann 22; Mary 1

Goode, Elizabeth 2

Gordon, Hannah 23; Sally 16;
Ursula 7

Grant, Jane 2

Graham, Mary E. 41

Green, Easter 11; Elizabeth
54; Franky Davis 51;
Lucetty 26; Lusey 47;
Martha 55; Mary Ann 20;
Nancy 28,78; Sarah 34,49,
56

Greenlaw, Mary 64

Gregory, Ann 52; Elizabeth 2;
Fanny 40; Lettice 2;
Martha 75; Martha L. 11;
Peggy 65; Polly 32; Sally
32; Susannah 2

Grinnan, Rockey 54; Sally 53

Griggs, Mary 24; Molley Spence
3; Nancy 50

Griffin, Margarett, 19

Griffis, Amiss 18

Grimes, Charity 70

Grisset, Polly 28

Gutridge, ---- 5; Ann 27;
Delia 57; Fanny 46; Jinny
53; Martha Ann 14; Mary
Ann 23; Milissa 49; Nancy
66; Peggy 34

Hail, Mary G. 76

Hallbrooks, Elizabeth 13,53;
Sarah 62

Hall, Alice 68; Amelia P. 37;
Anne 29; Ann Sanford 66;
Ellen 18; Elizabeth 5,45;
Frances 37; Jane H. 58;
Louisa H. 45; Martha 68;
Maria 54; Mary 41,69; Mary
Ann 61; Nancy 10,22,24,45;
Rachel 20; Sally 1,,64;
Sarah A. 27; Susan 38

Hammet, Verlinda 43

Hammans, Winney 77

Harper, Mary S. 75; Patty S. 29;
Sarah 74

Hart, Patty 14; Patsey 50

Harte, Mary 20

Hartly, Winifred 16

Harvey, Ann E. 65; Eliza B. 62;
Elizabeth J. 33; Lucy F. 59;
Lucinda 49; Mary Jett 67;
Virginia M. 25

Harris, Alice 5; Ann 46; Elizabeth 75; Mary 9; Molly 21;
Olivia 55;

Harrison, Agnes R. 30; Caty 5;
Easter 71; Eliza Ann 11;
Elizabeth 19,66; Hannah 45;
Jane R. 78; Judy 19; Martha
38; Mary 29,50; Mary P. 11;
Nancy 32; Sally 29

Harrington, Mary W. 23

Hardwick, Ellen P. 20; Elizabeth
4; Elizabeth R. 15

Hawkins, Louisa F. 68; Margarett
55, Molly 69; Peggy 8

Hawood, Winefret 32

Haynie; Helen H. 77

Hazard, Aggay 62; Ann N. 30;
Ann Eliza 67; Eliza A.
33; Lucy 15
Hazzard, Hadassah 58; Polly
40; Sally 20

Healy, Henrietta A. 28

Head, Ann 39; Leanah 36; Polly
51; Sally 58

Hedley; Sally 41

Henry, Letty 29

Henage, Elizabeth 9, Nancy 69;
Susan 6
Hennage, Fanny 6

Hewlet, Cloey 16

Hilliard, Fanny 39

Hillyard, Lucy 22

Hill, Elizabeth 49; Mary 35;
Nelly 44

Hines, Polly 10

Hinson, Ann 31; Betsey 35;
Caty 49, Eliza 15; Eliz-
abeth 69,70,76; Felicia
35; Harriott 49; Lucy 24,
73; Mary 8; Mary M. 31;
Molly 7; Sally 11,49,63;
Sarah 36; Shady 12,50;
Susan 27,31

Hipkins, Charlott 16, Elizabeth 16; Mary 23; Mary W.
16; Peggy 45

Hodge, Catherine Roberta Rose 3;
Hannah West 13; Sarah 76;

Holbrook, Fanny 62

Holliday, Julia Ann 12; Louisa
4
Hollinshead, Nelly 65

Holland, Rockey 33

Hopkins, Ellen 36

Hore, Fanney 67

Hoult, Thirza 67

How, Betsey 19

Howe, Polly 47

Howel, Alesy 32

Howell, Molly 64

Howson, Desty M. 2; Elizabeth 2; Fanny 26

Hubbard, Hannah 36

Hudson, Eliza B. 77; Elizabeth W. 24; Hannah Corbin 10; Julian 68

Hudnall, Betsy 52

Hueson, Mahaley 30

Hughs, Elizabeth 73;

Hughsencraft, Sally 76

Hull, Nancy 24

Hullums, Sally 15

Hunter, Ann 53; Ann P. 34; Emily Jane 78; Harriett H. 34; Sary P. 52; Susan P. 78

Hungerford, Ann W. 29

Hutchings, Elizabeth 60

Hutt, Elis M 15; Elizabeth 57; Mary Young 42

Hylard, Alice 11

I

Iles, Nancy 9

Ingham, Mary 34

Insley, Polly 44

J

Jacobs, Margaret 11

Jackson, Ellen 30; Eleanor 16; Elizabeth 23,66; Hannah 16; Mary 71, Polly 10,44; Rebecca Newton 71; Rockey 52; Sally 50; Susan 74

James, Delila 30; Eliza 71; Frances 35,45; Lucinda 35, 44; Maria 4; Margaret 20

Jeffery, Mary 14

Jeffries, Alice L. 52; Ann 15; Ann B. 22; Elizabeth 59; Fanny 1; Jane 34; Lucy 1; Mary Ann 48

Jennings, Frances 63

Jenkins, Ailcy 15; Ann 70,75; Bethuell 51; Betsy 43; Elizabeth 27; Fanny 55; Frances 17; Frances F. 23; Martha 37; Mary M. 20; Sally 77; Sarah 35; Sebina 28; Sebina B. 61; Susan 32; Winneyfrid 47

Jett, Ann 30; Catherine 49,65; Elizabeth 3,26,32,54; Frankey 40; Mary Ann Piper 22; Mary Jane 73; Molley 44; Nancy 68; Susan N. 57

Jewell, Keziah 8

Johnston, Ann F. 36

Johnson, Ann 9,61; Ann B. 9; Clara 70; Cornelia 13; Delitha 1; Elizabeth 53; Fanny 36,50; Frances Ann 12; Hannah 70; Harriet C. 9, Jenny 50; Juda 36; Kessey 14; Lucy 50; Mary 43; Meriah 14; Margarett

Caroline 50; Elizabeth 2,
66; Fanny 60; Frances 40;
Hannah 5,70; Joyce 78;
Julian 70; Kesiah 28; Louisa
54; Lucy 34; Margaret 21;
Mary Ann 70; Penny 7; Sillar
77;

Lune, Felitia 55

Luttrell, Fanny 18

Lyell, Fanny 35; Mary E. S. 9

M

McCance, Mary Jane 25

McCarty, Ann R. 39; Elizabeth
67, 5; Margaret 67

McCave, Fanny 3

McCay, Priscilla 14

McClannahan, Eliza J. 6;
Elizabeth 79; Jane E. 14
Magdaleñ. 28; Mary 54;
Nancy N. 33; Patty 44;
Rebecca 63; Sarah 24;

McCluskey, Susan 54

McCoy, Nancy 41

McDaniel, Amanda 19; Mary 19;
65

McGinniss, Rutho 61

McGuire, Alsey 42; Elizabeth 42,
58; Martha 1; Mary 56;
Polly 18

McGuy, Betsey 28; Catherine 71

McKave, Elizabeth 46

McKerney, Alice 69

McKenny, Caty 71; Dianna 61;
Flerder 38; Hannah 23;
Harriett 53; Molley 42;
Peggy 14

McKenney, Alice V. 42; Alice
42; Alice R. 78; Ann 39;
Barbary 35; Betsy 32;
Caty 46; Elizabeth 9;
Fanny 36; Frances 41,42;
Frances Y. 8; Jane 22;
Jemima 21; Lucinda B. 45;
Martha 58; Nancy 42; Sarah
8; Susannah 2

McKildoe, Juliana 76; Peggy S.
41

McKinney, Ann Maria 21; Ann M.
55; Mary W. 15; Sally 59;
Sarah 39

McKoy, Betsy 71

McKy, Polly 74

McNeale, Jane 45

McNeil, Harriott 3; Nancy 44

Macoy, Hannah 53

Mahorny, Lucy 21

Maith, Catherine A.R.J. 78

Mann, Hannah 26

Marks, Amy 70, Ann M. 9; Cath-
erine 43; Letta 66; Martha
A. 77; Mary 5; Nanny 31;
Peggy 63; Penelope 21
Sukey 63

Martin, Elizabeth P. 6; Jane
50; Janney 50; Margaret 31;

Mariner, Sarah 72

Marmaduke, Ann P. 33; Eliza-
beth 5,40,70; Fanny 32;
Frances 9; Keziah 40;
Lorinda Q. 40; Nancy 52;
Sarah 28

Marshall, Maria 7

Massey, Celia 47; Lucetta 36;
Mary 46; Patty 19

Maskiel, Elizabeth 26; Mary 11

Mathews, Jemima 59; Mary 78

Mathis, Mahala M. 57

Mathaney, Hannah 50

Mathany, Nancy 3

Maund, Anne Martin 2

Mazerean, Zalea Monzer 68

Mazarett, Margaret 25

Mealey, Fanny 1

Merchant, Cloe 64

Messick, Elizabeth 64

Mezick, Polly 73

Micon, Louisa 3

Middleton, Alice 6; Anne 24
Elizabeth 25,60; Frances 16;
Hannah 28; Hannah L. 56;
Judah 5; Louisa 30; Mary 16;
Martha 51; Moley 54; Molley F.
25

Miller, Elizabeth 25; Mahala 62;
Mary Jane 12; Margaret 50;
Pattey 49

Minor, Fanny 5; Frances 68

Mitchell, Betsy B♦ 35; Jane 76;
Martha 43; Maria 19; Olivia
Ann 44; Sally 49

Montgomery, Anne 73; Ahmaly 20;
Eliza Ann 55; Mary 55; Sarah
Ann 46

Monroe, Alice 78; Alice J. 36; Ann
59; Betsey 66; Catherine 7;
Susanna 67

Mongar, Susan 12

Moor, Amelia Ann 5

Moore, Elizabeth 39; Lucinda
51; Mary 14

Morris, Augilla 8; Catherine
57; Elizabeth 36,51; Fanny
57; Hannah 48; Mahala 45;
Mary 2.45; Peggy 68; Sally
55; Sarah 68; Susannah 41;

Morrison, Harriot 61

Morgan, Elizabeth B. 39; Mary
P. 73

Morton, Elizabeth 27; Sally
Sneed 27

Moreton, Caty 8

Morton, Hannah 58

Morrel, Elizabeth 19

Mors, Elizabeth 16

Morse, Elizabeth 38; Polly 60

Moss, Deborah 24

Mothershead, Alice or Sary 47;
Alice M. 49; Amelia 62;
Ann H. 43; Caty 46; Elisha
75; Elizabeth 19,34,70;
Elizabeth Ann 15; Elizabeth
A. 36; Fanny 56; Hannah C.
69; Jane S. 63; Julyett 37;
Julia Ann 41; Laurenda 54;
Leannah 75; Lucy 4,56;
Martha 44; Mary 46; Mary M.
29; Maria 77; Minerva J. 62;
Penny 1; Polly 5; Sally 9,
18; Sary E. 26; Susan 4

Moxley, Ann 34; Caty 65; Elizabeth 22,41; Elizabeth Muse
23; Frances 11; Lucy 43;
Mary S. 62; Nancy S. 45;
Patty 53; Peggy 25; Sally
2; Susanna 69

Mozengo, Nancy 24,58; Nelly 63;
Ruth 7; Sebey 61

Muir, Priscilla 5

O

Mullins, Elizabeth 4,9; Jane 9;
ary 65; Mary Ann 51; Nancey
22,23; Sarah Ann 51,69

O'Harrow, Martha 29

Oatis, Margaret Ann 23

Murry, Mary 27

Oldham, Martha 34, Sarah E.
68

Murphy, Ann 34; Ann Ballantine 60;
Eliza Ferguson 11; Eliza J. 59;
Sarah H. 18

Olliv, Sally 1

Muse, Betsy 20; Caty 27; Elinor
23; Eliza J. 3; Elizabeth 52;
Elizabeth D. 35; Lucy 49;
Mary 2,11; Margaret 47,65,71;
Molly 73; Nancy 32,35; Peggy
28,65; Rebecca 51; Sally 20;
Sophia 32; Susannah 10,45,49;
Susanna Maria 29

Olive, Molly 28, Nancy 2

Ollive, Catherine 1; Susannah
51

Oliff, Alcy 55; Fanny D. 15;
Jane 48; Lucy 78; Nancy
12; Sary Ann 61

Oliffe, Margaret A. 63

N

Omohundro, Ann 33,74; Dianna
Moss 50; Martha 34,40;
Mary Ann 28; Mary B. 28

Nash, Ann 71; Castella 78; Fanny
8; Jane 56,74; Kitty 69;
Lucy 53; Mary Ann 27; Mary A.
70; Martha 57; Susannah 21

Owens, Anne 65; Elizabeth 20;
Emily 17; Louisa Jane 26

Neale, Anne 53; Elizabeth 68; Frances 67; Hannah 4; Lucinda 45;
Mary Ann 31; Meriah 57; Mira
54; Nancy 50; Sally 13

Owen, Jane 45

P

Nelson, Alice 29; Ann 72; Ann E. 22;
Betsy 35; Elizabeth 69; Frances
32; Jane 71; Sally 77; Susannah
76

Packett, Elizabeth S. 73;
Nancy 69

Palmer, Eliza 57; Elizabeth
8; Elizabeth D. 17;
Sally 16; Sarah 20

Nevitt, Sarah 53

Parmer, Elizabeth 10

Newman, ---- 63; Eliza 70; Elizabeth
55; Fanny 63; Grace 71; Judy 3;
Martha 64; Martha F. 63; Rachel
12

Paris, Sarah 7

Parress, Mary 4

Newton, Eliza B. 48; Sally 62; Sally
B. 66

Parker, Elizabeth 17,53;
E. Maria 69; Frances 7;
Hannar 65; Henrietta 48;
Judith B. 72; Juliet O.
17

Newgent, Betty 3

Northern, Molley F. 59

Parks, Bridget 6; Polly 33;
Sarah A. M. 6

Norwood, Betsy 17; Mary 3

Partridge, Jemima 64

Payne, Eliza A. 19; Elizabeth
C. 44; Mary 17; Ursley 38;
Winifred L. 34

Payton, Ann 21; Jane 37; Lucinda 34; Molly 13

Peake, Catherine 53; Mary E. 38

Peck, Anne Tasker 56; Mary Ann
25; Sarah S. 58

Pecure, Susanna 18

Peed, Abby 39; Caty 31; Eliza
47; Jane 57; Mary 63; Maria
39; Sarah 8

Pegg, Felicia 4

Peirce, Ann 9,12; Betsy 77;
Fanny 14; Mary E. 45; Marg-
aret G. 30; Martha 30; Sally
R. 26

Pendergrass, Kesiah 47

Pilliam, Mary 38; Sally 27

Pillman, Polly 66

Pillsbury, Mary 41

Pinkard, Elizabeth 53

Pitts, Harriett 27; Sarah J.
43; Sarah E. 72

Pitman, Frances James 10

Playl, Anne 63

Plummer, Elizabeth 4; Sarah
A. J. 40

Pomroy, Ann 7

Poor, Ann C. 1; Harriet 18;
Mary 2

Poosy, Nancy 23

Pope, Caty 67 (see Sanford)

Pope, Frankey 21; Jane Carter
56; Jenny 40; Martha 4;
Mary 12; Sarah 36

Porter, Betty 61; Elenor 25;
Mary Ann 41; Mary A. 43;
Sally 51

Potter, Alice B. 42; Sarah 36

Preits, Caty 18

Price, Ann 77

Pridham, Mary Ann 32

Pritchett, Priscilla 17

Pullin, Eleanor 51; Susanna
34

Pumroy ---- 70; Elizabeth 70;
Molly 67; Nancy 78

Pursley, Ann 27; Betsy 28;
Jane 75; Mahala Ann 48;
Mary 28,37; Martha 39;
Sally 27

Pursell, Mary A. 59

Q

Quisenbury, Alice 6; Ann 18;
Catherine 43,58; Mary 75;
Margaret 5; Nancy 47

R

Ramey, Elizabeth 46; Fanny
Lewis 30

Randolph, Sally Lee 16

Randall, Aggay 77

Rawlet, Ann 34

Ray, Nancy C. 4

Reamy, Adelaide T. 45; Adeline
62; Baynton B. 27; Carlisle
E. 4; Delia 12; Eliza 27;

Elizabeth 70; Kitty 74;
Mahaley A. 34; Mary 63;
Nancy 12, 20; Sally 53;
Sarah A. 51

Reade, Ailcey 17

Redman, Elizabeth 16,52; Eliza-
beth A. 30; Frances 59,73;
Harriot W. 36; Jane E. 60;
Jemima 77; Lucy 66; Mary S.
65; Martha F. 6; Molly 36;
Molly P. 33; Naney R. 58;
Sally A. 33; Susan R. 69

Redeck, Elizabeth 4

Reed, Mary Muse 29

Reynolds, Elizabeth 7,55,61,63;
Lorinda 58; Mary 29; Molley
49

Rice, Ann R. 8; Frankey 60;
Hannah 15; Jemima 17;
Letty A. 22; Mary R. 11;
Mary T. 11

Richardson, Eliza M. 72; Elizabeth T. 47; Nancy 8

Riels, Elizabeth 56

Riggs, Sabinah 58

Riley, Ann 31; Elizabeth 47;
Elizabeth W. 13; Jane 41;
Mary 62; Sally 47

Ringmaden, Ann Rice 30;

Ringmaiden, Moley Martin 35

Robinson, Ann 5,18,32; Ann S.
34; Ann Washington 60;
Elizabeth 8; Frances 57;
Frances M. 58; Hannah 48;
Keziah 68; Mary 13,71;
Mary C. 58; Margaret 41;
Molley 60; Nancy 69;
Sally 38,73; Sally M. 62;
Sally A. 57; Sarah 40;
Sarah R. 69; Susan R. 31;
Ursia P. 60

Robb, Lucy 73

Roe, Fanny 31, Sarah 3

Rowe, Elizabeth 69

Ross, Winnefer 39

Rose, Bethlehem 13; Eliza 47;
Elizabeth 42; Ethelenda 36;
Frances F. 75; Jane E. 47;
Jane P. 74; Mary S. 15;
Mildred W. 60; Sabina 61;
Sarah 28

Rowand, Judith B. 71

Rust, Elizabeth 13; Elizabeth L.
27; Hannah 6; Jane R. 5;
Mary 77; Winifrid C. 6

Ryall, Eliza 51

Ryalls, Sally 17

Ryals, Sary 51

Ryls, Susannah 26

S

Sale, Hannah 70; Isabella 50

Sampson, Catherine 47; Fanny 57·
Mary Susan 30; Sally 57

Sanford, Alice R. 55; Ann 16;
Ann E. 18; Ann M. 1; Bettey
42; Caty 42,67(see Pope);
Elizabeth 8,19,23,49,73;
Eliza 62; Fanny 64; Franky 23;
Frances 13,64; Hannah 29;
Jane 1; Jemima 61,68; Lovin-
da 62; Lucy 40,57; Nancy 14;
Peggy 52,61; Penelope 13;
Penny 74; Polly 3; Rachel
28; Sarah 66; Susan 14;
Sukey 37; Susannah 31;
Ursley 39

Sandford, Bethiah 31; Caty 78;
Frances 6; Mary M. 14;
Peggy 35; Sarah Jane 32;
Susanna W. 65

Sandy, Dorotha 78; Elizabeth 65;
Isabell 28; Mary 55; Polly 9

Sanders, Alice 8, Elizabeth 2;
Jane 12,65; Mary Lewis 7;
Margaret 12; Rachel 34; Susan
37; Susanna 61
Saunders, Judah 62

Scales, Sarah 43; Sophia 33

Scinner, Sarah 12

Scott, Patsy Hammock 38; Rebecca
51; Sally 54;

Scutt, Jimima 13; Patty 28

Seader, Kesiah 59

Self, Ann 46,72; Caty 22; Eliza-
beth 20,71; Elizabeth B. 52;
Elizabeth M. 37; Eliza M. 64;
Hannah 4,26; Jane Middleton
38; Martha R. 15; Margaret 9,
40; Mary 53,77; Milly 64;
Molly 22; Polly 42; Nancy
Beal 6; Patty 2; Polly 29;
Sally S. 60; Susan 9; Susan
B. 29

Selvey, Sarah 34

Settle, Charlotte 38, Jane 35

Shackleford, Nancy 20

Shadrack, Betsy 28

Shadrick, Mary 30

Shirly, Elizabeth 18; Frances 38

Short, Alcey 21; Catherine 70;
Margarett 1 ,49; Pheby 35;
Sarah Elizabeth 45; Winney
39

Shoats, Elizabeth 57

Sylvia(Silva,Silba,Silby) Sally
31; Susanna 40; Ann 28;
Elizabeth 28; Sally 77

Sims, Sally 35

Simms, Felicia 37; Jane 52;
Mary 35; Susan 14
Simmes, Elizabeth 52

Simpson, Eliza 9

Simkins, Sarah 38

Sisson, Ann S. 22, Ann 46;
Eliza M. 16; Frances 58;
Patty 55; Peggy 42; Sally
48,66; Winny 67

Smoote, Elizabeth 10

Sorrel, Susan 3

Spark, Lucy S. 9; Polly 14

Spence, Ann 9,62; Amelia 32;
Betsy 8; C. C. 54; Eliza-
beth B. 17; Jemima 17,58;
Mary A. 14,32; Margaret 42;
Sally 72

Spilman, Elizabeth 49; Eliza J.
72; Elizabeth 65; Jane 47;
Nancy 12,27; Olivia A. 25

Spurling, Ann 30; Frances 2;
Martha 6; Maria 20,65;
Malinda 12; Milley 10;
Sally 28; Sally B. 23

Smith, Ann 65; Barbary 30;
Catherine 39; Charlotte 73;
Eliza Ann 15; Eliza T. 19;
Elizabeth 48; Elender Lord
58; Fanney 18,40; Frances
16; Hannah Bushrod 8;
Hannah 46; Jane 4; Lucy 5,
29; Maria 7; Margaret A. 21
Mary 15,50,53,55,75; Mary
F. 22; Mary M. 66; Mary S.
64; Peggy 36; Rachel C. 45;
Rose 50; Sally 77; Sally B.
13; Sarah 66; Susan 20;
Susannah 5

Smither, Mary Ann 63, Susan E.
48
Steel, Elizabeth 8; Ellenor
31

V

VanNess, Ann M. 75; Emeline 14

Vaughan, Mary 59

Vigar, Elizabeth 72; Frances
    Bayne 20; Peney 54
Villard, Constance U. E. 33

W

Walker, Ann 64; Elizabeth 51;
    Elizabeth B. 49; Eliza S.
    62; Frances 67; Jane F. 16;
Wallace, Juliet A. 1

Wann, Ann C. 74

Wane, Lucy L. 78

Waring, Eliza L. 24

Washington, Alice Bailey 24;
    Ann 22,62; Betsey 57; Caty
    31; Elizabeth 53; Frances
    27,73; Jemima 34; Leanner
    18; Lucy 19; Martha 49;
    Mildred 39; Nancy 40,59,60;
    Sarah 56; Sarah F. 73;
    Sibella 31
Watson, Ann 69; Elizabeth 63;
    Sarah A. 9
Waughan, Sibby 38

Weaver, Alice 13,74; Ann 37;
    Ann M. 48; Eliza J. 29;
    Elizabeth 25,37,43,61;
    Fanney 2; Frances 60,63;
    Harriot 61; Henrietta 19;
    Letty 54; Lucinda 19,48;
    Mary 61, Nancy 18; Polly
    17; Prissilley 14; Sebinah
    14; Susan Ann 57; Susannah
    59
Weadon, Fanny 31

Webb, Elizabeth A. 65

Weedon, Elizabeth 10

Weeks, Elizabeth 4, Lucy 3;
    Mary 52; Polly 52
Weldon, Elizabeth 72; Frankey
    57; Lucy 43; Mary 48; Priscy
    2; Sally 47

Weston, Amey 15

Whearitt, Nancy 50

Wheeler, Eliza 6; Maria 8;
    Polly 52;
Whealer, Mary 38

White, Anne 27; Catharine 35;
    Charlotte 56; Elizabeth 19;
    Felicia 49; Frances 69; Jane
    35; Nancy 17,24
Whitley, Alcey 65

Whoosencroft, Hannah 31

Wigley, Polly

Wilkins, Ann Margaret 56; Eliz-
    abeth 26; Polly B. 39
Wilkerson, Ann 38

Wilson, Lucy 62; Mary 44,62;
    Maria 11; Martha 55;
    Nancy 20,23; Rebecca 55;
    Sally 5,76; Sarah 1; Susan
    7; Winifred 68
Williams, Calvert S. 26; Hannah
    36; Magdalen 18; Margaret
    48; Mary 71,74; Nancy 25,
    26; Sarah Ann 52
Wills, Sarah 15

Winkfield, Jane 27,33m73;
    Susanna 28
Winstead, Susanner 19
Winstead, Louisa 9

Withers, Olivia 61

Wood, Frances 10; Mary 10

Woosoncroft, Sarah T. 17
Worsencraft, Hannah 31

Worney,Eliza 15

Worth, Anne 18

Wright, Aggatha 5; Agathy 14;
    Ann M. 59; Elizabeth S; Eliz-
    abeth C. 34; Hannah 73; Jane
    M. 6; Mary C. 55; Mary E. 79;
    Mary P. 59; Mary W. 7

Wroe, Alice 37; Elizabeth 32,44;
 Fanny 9; Frances 13,24; Hannah 45;
 Polly 46

Y

Yardley, Ellen 7; Jane 40; Nancy 48;
 Winney 56

Yeatman, Amelia S. 70; Catherine M. 28;
 Eliza Ann 16; Elizabeth 30,62;
 Fanny 54; Lucy 35,51; Mary 17; Nancy B. 2;
 P---ty 61; Sally 71

Young, Margaret 8

www.ingramcontent.com/pod-product-compliance
Lightning Source LLC
Chambersburg PA
CBHW070929270326
41927CB00011B/2789